The
Arthritic's
Cookbook

The Arthritic's Cookbook

Collin H. Dong, M.D.
and Jane Banks

GRANADA
London Toronto Sydney New York

Published by Hart-Davis, MacGibbon Ltd 1974
Second impression 1975
Third impression 1975
Fourth impression 1976
Fifth impression 1978
Sixth impression 1978
Seventh impression published by Granada Publishing 1979
Eighth impression 1979
Ninth impression 1979

Granada Publishing Limited
Frogmore, St Albans, Herts AL2 2NF
and
3 Upper James Street, London W1R 4BP
866 United Nations Plaza, New York, NY 10017, USA
117 York Street, Sydney, NSW 2000, Australia
100 Skyway Avenue, Rexdale, Ontario, M9W 3A6, Canada
PO Box 84165, 2034 Johannesburg, South Africa
CML Centre, Queen & Wyndham, Auckland 1, New Zealand

Copyright © Collin H. Dong and Jane Banks 1973
ISBN 0 246 10818 5

Printed in Great Britain by
Richard Clay (The Chaucer Press), Ltd,
Bungay, Suffolk

Granada Publishing ®

To Jerome Taylor

Contents

Introduction

Arthritis is a malady that conjures up in our mind's eye a picture of a crotchety old man sitting in a wheelchair; his every movement is painful and awkward. Invariably he holds a pair of crutches or a cane in his knobby, clawlike hands to aid him in making short trips from his home base, the wheelchair.

At the age of thirty-five, after practising medicine for seven years, I was afflicted with this baffling disease. For three years, the only relief from the agony of this disorder was taking large doses of aspirin and other related analgesics ordered by my doctors.

After consulting and being treated by many specialists, locally and elsewhere, my arthritis became progressively worse. In addition to the racking pains in my various joints, I developed a generalized dermatitis. My last consultant, like all the others, was in a quandary. He told me that there was nothing he could suggest for further treatment of these two diseases, my arthritis and my skin problem. His final advice was to see a psychiatrist.

I knew that I was slowly going crazy, but I wanted to think that I was not yet ready for a head shrinker. Needless to say, after the last pronouncement I had a soul-searching and sleepless night. But it also happened to be a fateful one, for when I looked into the mirror the next morning, I saw an appalling, repulsive reflection. That image shocked me into a new consciousness – not unlike an electric-shock treatment by a psychiatrist. The man in this reflected image had lost most of his black curly hair and was almost bald. The smooth yellow skin of his face was inflamed, swollen, cracked, and caked with a weeping exudate. His eyebrows were scanty, and his slanty eyelids were puffy and showed only a small slit of the eyes. He could barely lift his hands to wash his face due to the excruciating pain and stiffness in his shoulders. This was me! A physician who had been trained in modern medicine and who had been under the medical care of his most prominent colleagues.

During the three years of this illness I had read all the scientific papers, books, and journals dealing with the treatment of arthritis and its related diseases. The medical world up to that moment had not found the cause of arthritis and had no cure for this problem. Every rheumatologist whom I had consulted gave the same treatment that was outlined in the medical books and journals, and I had passively accepted their advice and therapy. Now they had given up my case. I was on my own. I was faced with the problem of finding some means of therapy to alleviate this ailment if I was not to be assigned to one of those wheelchairs for the rest of my life.

My traditional education and indoctrination had conditioned my mind to accept without question the teachings of the famous physicians I consulted. Now I was confronted with an emergency – a sink-or-swim situation. I had heard stories of a drowning man grasping at straws and how his whole life history flashed through his mind an instant before unconsciousness. Although I was not drowning, something similar happened to me. I also had a flashback with an instant recall of my past life.

What I remembered most vividly at that moment was my father saying to me, as he said to all his nine children whenever any of us became ill: *Bing chung how yup, woh chung how chut*. Literally translated this means, 'Sickness enters through the mouth, and catastrophe comes out of the mouth.'

I had forgotten this sage folk observation in my pursuit of Western higher education and scientific knowledge. Now that all the expertise had failed me, I was grasping at straws.

Incredible as it may sound, this axiom was the straw that eventually rescued me from a wheelchair. This old adage pointed me in another direction. Perhaps I had been putting some 'sickness' through my mouth for a long time without realizing it.

For up to this very moment, I had given very little consideration to the problem of nutrition and its effect on the human body, except that I knew I had to eat to live and work. Throughout my life I had been on a more or less simple Chinese diet consisting mainly of beef, pork, chicken, fish, vegetables, and rice. When I started the practice of medicine in 1931, I gradually changed to a diet like that of most affluent Americans. The reason for this transition has been suggested by Dr S. I. Hayakawa, in his great book *Symbol, Status, and Personality*: 'Advertising spends untold millions to build up connotations, to teach us to put implicit faith in the affective overtones with which "brand names" are invested. . . . Advertising, as currently practised, is almost entirely a matter of pound, pound, pounding into people word-mindedness to the exclusion of fact-mindedness.'

Being a busy practitioner, this subliminal propaganda produced by the dream-factories of Madison Avenue compelled me to eat brand A orange juice and fruit; brand B milk and ice cream; brand C bacon, eggs, beef, pork, chicken, and lamb; brand D vegetables, green and yellow, brand E bread and cereals.

How can such a wonderfully balanced diet make anyone sick? Every book on diet and nutrition written by famous doctors, dietitians, or nutritionists recommends just such a diet. Yet I was crippled with two chronic diseases that defied the attempts of the scientific medical practitioners to cure. Little did I know that I was also afflicted with a third disease, 'word-mindedness'.

Generally in a crisis the instincts come to the rescue. It happened here too – 'fact-mindedness' suddenly entered my confused mentality. I started questioning the validity of the

11

advice and writings of brand-name authorities. After all, I was descended from a culture that was 6,000 years old and from people who had never had any brand-name foods.

Their daily sustenance for thousands of years has been the basic ingredients that nature gave to all the people of the universe – meat, vegetables, rice, or wheat.

The past history of my immediate family, nine brothers and sisters and my parents, had always manifested a high degree of allergy to foods: father to pork; Dr Eugene to wheat and milk; Ella and Alice to turkey and melon; Dr Hubert to eggs; Harriet to seafood; Lily to green leafy vegetables; Dr Emma to tomatoes and milk; and Dr Marion to seafood and oranges. Mother, with her peaches-and-cream complexion, was not allergic to anything. However, I, Collin, the glutton of the family, was allergic to milk, wheat, eggs, and fruit – especially oranges.

Allergy to food has been chronicled in Chinese medical literature for many centuries. The aphorism 'Sickness enters through the mouth and catastrophe comes out of the mouth' was no doubt originally propagated by the first emperor of China, Shen Nung. He ordered pregnant women to stop eating shellfish because it caused *fung non*, which we call hives or urticaria. He reasoned that if shellfish can cause poisoning of the skin, it could cause ill effects on the unborn child. Horse meat was another forbidden food, because it was thought that it caused miscarriages.

With these salient facts in mind – the dictum of Emperor Shen Nung, the past history of my family, and the arthritis that had baffled the doctors – I launched myself on what we would call a 'poor man's diet', comprising simple meat, vegetables, and rice. I also continued to use a variety of medications and ointments to ease my symptoms.

At first the experimental efforts were not rewarding, but gradually, by eliminating certain medications, especially aspirin, and different food components in my diet, I began feeling a general improvement. I discovered that there and

12

then the most satisfactory diet for my arthritis was a combination of seafood, vegetables, and rice.

To my utter amazement, in a few short weeks there was a metamorphosis. I was able to sleep again, for the fitful nightmares of years were gone. I was able to shave again, for the skin became soft and pliable and did not 'weep'. I was agile again, for I went from 195 lb to 150 lb. I was able to play golf again, for the stiffness and pain in my joints disappeared. I was able to smile again, for the psychological torture of years was alleviated. I had almost a complete remission from my crippling disease.

This remission has miraculously lasted for thirty-four years. On my next birthday I shall be seventy-three years of age. Every morning I play either nine or eighteen holes of golf, or I practise hitting four to five hundred golf balls and I pick them up myself. My golf score will vary from the high seventies to the low eighties, depending upon how much I am betting with Charlie Lazzari.

Every three to six months I take a blood test. Last week the test was within normal limits. My electrocardiograph was normal. The gastrointestinal series indicated that I had a healed duodenal ulcer. No doubt it had been incurred during my illness more than thirty years ago.

Today my life-style and daily routine, in addition to my golf, consists of making morning rounds at the hospital and answering the complaints of residents in two large blocks of flats. In the afternoon I treat from thirty to forty patients five days a week. After office hours I make occasional house calls if necessary, or attend corporation and hospital staff meetings.

My present diet is now restricted to fish, vegetables, and rice. I sleep soundly for about five to six hours every night. My one indulgence in life is that I have a chauffeur to drive me to and from work, and house calls. The driver is my beautiful, patient, and talented wife. Her remuneration is an annual adventurous holiday to faraway places around the globe.

13

My dramatic recovery convinced me that one of the causes of rheumatic diseases is allergy to food and additives. Upon returning to my medical practice, I incorporated a diet in addition to the usual chemical therapy for all my patients. I give them a lecture on the subject of nutrition in relation to health and illness. I warn them against the hazards of eating processed and prepared foods containing artificial flavouring, colouring, chemical preservatives, and other additives. The rewards of these few minutes of conversation with the patient are immeasurable in getting their cooperation and confidence.

In the past thirty years I have treated thousands of cases of rheumatic diseases. The high percentage of remissions from pain and misery with my method is remarkable. I have been asked by my many patients why I did not disseminate my knowledge to help others. Why was a book not written?

The answer is a simple one. I did not have the courage to fight the medical establishment. We live in a world where it takes many years to build one's professional reputation. My method of treatment is an empirical one. It was not established on a scientific or theoretical basis accepted by the medical world.

As an example of what has to be disproved and disputed, let me quote a booklet I was given when I recently attended an eight-hour seminar on rheumatic diseases. The pamphlet is titled *The Truth About Diet and Arthritis*, and is issued by the Arthritis Foundation. Its first statement is: 'There is no special diet for arthritis. No specific food has anything to do with causing it. And no specific diet will cure it.' Further on, the pamphlet states: 'The fact is, the possibility that some dietary factor either causes or can help control arthritis has been thoroughly and scientifically investigated and disproved. The only exceptions are in gout.' These authoritative, arbitrary, and tyrannical words were issued on an expensive, beautifully printed, brown, blue, and white paper by the Arthritis Foundation.

I would have accepted the validity of these promulgations

14

without question if, in the first place, the remission of my arthritic affliction had not lasted more than thirty years, and, secondly, if my painful symptoms had not recurred whenever I deviated from my diet – and, finally, if the thousands of patients with arthritis that I have treated over the years had not had such dramatic relief from their pain and suffering.

Furthermore, another piece of literature issued by the Arthritis Foundation, *Diet and Arthritis – A Handbook for Patients*, states:

> *But there is overwhelming evidence that nutritionally balanced meals eaten regularly benefit anyone's overall health, muscle tone, and in the case of arthritis, build ability to resist the wear and tear of the disease ... in general the good diet for anyone, whether you have arthritis or not, is based on a selection from four food groups. Briefly, they are the milk group, the meat group, the vegetable and fruit group, and the bread and cereal group.*

In other words arthritic sufferers should eat anything and everything they find in the local food markets and plenty of it. Yet there is overwhelming evidence that serious illnesses and even catastrophe result from eating certain food components. Dr Jean Mayer, professor of nutrition at Harvard University, writes: 'Ten-year-old Michael Gryzybinski died. That's right, died – from an anaphylactic reaction due to ingested peanuts.' This death was due to angioedema of the larynx, or, in common terms, asphyxiation due to the swelling of the throat caused by an allergic reaction after eating peanuts.

Information about and case histories of serious diseases caused by allergy is frequently published. It is estimated that vast numbers of people are suffering from some form of allergic disease, and perhaps one-quarter of them are seriously ill without being correctly diagnosed and treated. Moreover, in the study of allergies it has been found that

15

any item of food mentioned in the four recommended groups by the Arthritis Foundation can be allergens, the substances that cause the allergies.

The most common category of nutritional components is the milk group. But there is such a thing as milk intolerance, increasingly understood by the scientists. Practically every recipe in a normal diet contains small or large amounts of milk or milk powder. However, Theodore Bayless, M.D., of the Johns Hopkins University School of Medicine, says: 'Among white adults of Scandinavian or Western European extraction only 2 to 8 per cent are lactose intolerant ... in sharp contrast to the 60 to 80 per cent prevalence in samples of Greek Cypriots, Arabs, and Ashkenazi Jews, 70 per cent among American Negroes.'

This means that many thousands of people are allergic to milk. In the light of this report, the recommendation of milk or milk products to arthritics could hinder or complicate the recovery from this disease.

Such emphatic statements as the one quoted earlier – 'The fact is, the possibility that some dietary factor either causes or can help control arthritis has been thoroughly and scientifically investigated and disproved' – are not only unwarranted but discourage further research.

Let me ask, Who were the people who did all this research? What is their background? Are they just doctors, nutritionists, and dietitians sitting in a weekly conference, smoking their cigarettes and stuffing themselves with breakfasts, luncheons, and dinners served to them contaminated with preservatives, artificial flavouring and colouring, and monosodium glutamate?

If any of these research groups wish to investigate the nutritional aspect of the etiology of arthritis, let me make a suggestion! Ask for volunteers among the group of dedicated rheumatologists who are willing to spend a few months of their lives to go into food-processing factories and the kitchens of restaurants, hotels, convalescent homes, and sandwich makers to see how the food is prepared and what chemicals are added to preserve it, colour it, or make it taste better for the consumer. Then if they wish to investigate further, they should go into the slaughterhouses and watch how the meats are prepared and what is done with the leftovers and the various organs of the animals, which eventually become hot dogs, luncheon meats, and sausages. Then, and only then, can they say, 'Dietary factors have been thoroughly investigated.' And if among the investigating team there should be one who is afflicted with arthritis, his opinion will bear more weight.

At this juncture, let me warn my readers that diet alone will not cure arthritis or any other disease. I do not rule out medication. But medication alone will not cure diseases either. What I am suggesting is a radically modified diet supplemented by whatever moderate medication may be necessary in the individual case. And in evaluating diet, one must not forget that an affluent society consumes many highly advertised foods, food components, and preservatives, any of which can be allergenic. Eliminating these possible allergens should benefit everybody, especially the sick.

The fish diet that I recommend to my arthritic patients has been clinically shown to be effective in combination with medication. The bulletin issued by the U.S. Department of the Interior, September 1961, supports its value as a substitute for the usual beef, lamb, and pork proteins in any diet. This bulletin states:

Fish can be consumed three times daily due to its nutritional values, and in general is applicable to any diets designed to yield (1) needed biologically valuable trace minerals, (2) high levels of vitamins, especially those of the B complex system, (3) reduction of sodium intake and consequent reduction in body water retention, (4) reduction in hard fat intake and restoration of fatty acid balance between hard and soft fats, (5) high levels of readily available biologically complete, easily digestible

17

proteins, and (6) increase in body energy food intake with maximum ease of metabolic utilization.

The following scientific evidence is in support of my hypothesis that arthritis is an allergic disease: (1) As early as 1967 Dr Robert Good of the University of Minneapolis Medical School found that '... in patients who are unable to make gamma globulin and antibodies, arthritis is thirty times more common than it is in the general population.' (2) Recently Dr David Mumford of the Baylor College of Medicine, Houston, Texas, stated: 'New information about the two-part immune system has opened up the study of immunoglobulin, large molecules that are prototype antibodies. So far, we know about five of these. If one is lacking, for instance, it may lead to severe allergies. If another is not present, the body may have no defence against a whole variety of infectious diseases.'

The interpretation of these two scientific findings, which are emphatically in support of my concept, is that arthritis patients lack the ability to produce immunoglobulin or antibodies to protect themselves against allergens which cause the arthritis. I have found that my dietary regimen with medication, the objective of which is to eliminate the allergens, is clinically effective in the treatment of arthritis.

However, before anyone considers himself an arthritic, the disease should be diagnosed by a competent physician. Then, with his aid and direction, I am sure that you will benefit by changing your own confused nutritional pattern to one that is logical and practical.

– Collin H. Dong, M.D.
San Francisco

1

It Works for Me

I was one of the 40 million arthritics in the United States. In fact, I was fast becoming one of the 13 million disabled or crippled arthritics in the United States. I came by it naturally, as the saying goes. There is a familial history of arthritis and related diseases, such as gout. (Gout is rare in women, although I have it.) I had a severely crippled brother who died from the effects of a medication for rheumatoid arthritis, so I was understandably wary of the drugs being prescribed by the numerous doctors I progressed through in my search for help.

I was born an optimist; I felt sure that somewhere there was another answer to my problem, something more reasonable than fifteen aspirin a day plus the gamble of the cortisone-derivative drugs. The answer came, as it so often does, through a friend. Observing my stiff, painful movements and my swollen, knotty hands, he said, 'Jane, we had a man in our factory who was cured of arthritis.'

'Cured?' I said. 'But that's impossible!'

'Perhaps it's not a cure in the strictest sense,' my friend explained, 'but six months ago he was very nearly unable to work. He's an upholsterer, and his hands were so stiff he couldn't use them. Today he's fine, perfectly normal. He's been under treatment by Dr Dong, a Chinese doctor.'

Remember, I was in sad shape. I was unable to open my hands completely, I had a persistent pain in one hip, and the large joint of one foot was at times too painful for a shoe. We had recently bought a house on a beautiful lagoon because I love to swim; the pain in my shoulders made swimming impossible. Is it any wonder I literally leapt at my friend's suggestion?

Through him I received an appointment with the doctor. His office, with its Chinese decor, seemed quite foreign; I found him very charming. He was lean and fit with quick, precise movements; he looked about forty-five, but I learned later he is almost seventy.

'Tell me everything you eat in a day,' was his first demand. I outlined what I considered an extremely healthy high-protein, low-calorie diet consisting mainly of meat, eggs, and cheese.

'No wonder,' he said, shaking his head. 'From now on you will eat only fish and vegetables. Later we'll add an occasional breast of chicken. That is,' he added, 'if you want to stay well.'

'But,' I asked, 'does such a simple, restricted diet give you all the nutrients you need?'

'Let me explain it this way. The basis of foods is meat, vegetables, and starch. The amount consumed depends on the individual; actually he should be eating only to replace the breaking-down process of the body. He needs protein, vegetables, and carbohydrates – the protein to replace cells, the vegetables for minerals and vitamins. A diet restricted to these elements will slow down the ageing process in addition to increasing the life span. Incidentally,' he added, 'life is a paradox. When we are young and can tolerate the rich foods, most of us cannot afford them; when you can afford them your body no longer can handle the fats and spices.'

'Is that why so many people have arthritis?'

'Naturally an unwise diet will have varying adverse effects. However, arthritis and its related diseases are all too often the result.' He went on to explain that most people lose about ten pounds in the first week of the treatment, due to the high-protein, low-calorie characteristic of the diet. 'Vegetables and oils have a most beneficial effect on skin

20

tone,' he added. 'However, additives, preservatives, and spices are not necessary to body functioning.'

For the first time in many months I began to feel hopeful. However, I love to eat, and love to cook. I felt somewhat dismayed at what I considered a dreary culinary prospect. 'Isn't it awfully boring?' I asked.

'Not at all. With a little ingenuity you can make it a gourmet affair. Using the basic acceptable ingredients, plus vegetable oils and margarine, you'll find you can come up with some highly satisfying and tempting dishes. You'll have rice, of course, but go easy on refined white flour, whole grains, and cereals. You'll learn to be a careful label reader and find the brands of things that are acceptable. For instance, I recently discovered a delicious natural wheat bread containing no additives or preservatives. There are more and more natural foods available, thanks to the young.'

'You make it all sound so simple,' I said. 'It's almost too good to be true!'

Two weeks later I was almost completely free of pain, and now, after four years, I find it hard to remember exactly what it was like. The swelling disappeared gradually, and the stiffness with it. It seems to me I simply woke up one morning and realized I wasn't stiff any more. I feel absolutely marvellous now, and lead a completely normal life again. What is normal for me is a little more active than for the average woman my age; in addition to having a career – interior design – and a heavy schedule of entertaining, I do all the housework and take care of a rather extensive and demanding garden. I have a long swim every day, in season, and on weekends my husband and I take long rides on our racing bicycles. I have twice as much energy as I did ten years ago, and one by one my friends are capitulating to my diet just because I *look* so much better than I did ten years ago. I'm thin, my hair is shiny, and my skin has a good healthy colour; I'm more than happy about it all and totally committed to a lifetime of eating to stay that way.

21

(An incidental note might be added here; on my last visit to the dentist to have my teeth cleaned I was a source of immense interest to the technician. Everyone's gums bleed when scraped and prodded, but the technician called in the dentist to tell him she had never seen such tough gums, such nonbleeders. When I suggested that my diet might have something to do with it, my dentist nodded happily and agreed that this was undoubtedly the case.)

However, I do not claim this diet will *cure* you; obviously such claims can be made only after long research and documentation. I do know the diet worked for me, and for many, many other people, and if your symptoms are alleviated it will make me very happy.

I'm no medical expert, but I believe one of the reasons this works is because the body is getting what nature intended it to have in the first place. Sound, proper nutrition means furnishing the body with all the vitamins and minerals it needs; proper nutrition should also mean that the body is protected from poisons.

The fact that there are 40 million arthritics in the United States, according to the Arthritis Foundation, certainly has something to do with the increasingly deteriorating diet of the past few generations: an increase in foods from which all the value has been processed, foods treated with preservatives and additives that in some cases have been proven to be extremely dangerous.

All arthritic patients are by now well aware of the hard fact that there is as yet no positive cure for arthritis. However, medical research has made strides in proving that the human life span could be expanded twenty to forty years by limiting the intake of starch, sugar, dairy products, and meat. Long-term studies of diet and ageing have shown that the person who cuts his calorie intake 60 per cent by avoiding the above-listed foods is more resistant to disease and has a longer, more vigorous life. Also there is evidence that eliminating white refined flour and sugar has had a therapeutic effect on many arthritics. Incidentally, Sam, our

22

Labrador retriever, had developed arthritis in his hip. I took him off his huge daily ration of cooked meat and started giving him only kibbled grain, plus leftover fish and vegetables with tablespoons of corn oil. His limp disappeared almost immediately; shortly thereafter I discovered a high-protein grain product that enabled me to cut down on his calories, and now we have a lean, healthy, shiny dog again. It's the same story as with humans; as a young dog he could tolerate the diet, but as age changed his body it became necessary to make adjustments.

By now my enthusiasm for and faith in this regime must be apparent to you. Very recently I experienced a reaffirmation of this faith and enthusiasm as a result of a trip I took to the Far East. This book was completed, my husband was going to be away on a business trip, and since I had never been to the Orient, I decided the moment had come. I went to Hong Kong, Bangkok, and Singapore, and in each place found something to further strengthen my belief in this basically Oriental diet.

Although the pursuit of beauty and culture was the aim of the trip, I somehow found it to be a 'people trip'. The Chinese, thought-provoking as they are, certainly demonstrate the efficacy of their diet. However, I found the latter most dramatically demonstrated in Thailand. The people are most beautiful and seem to radiate good health and friendly spirit. Making the boat trips along the *klongs*, one wonders how these extremely impoverished people can be so healthy – that is, until one remembers that they live on fish and their fertile soil produces vegetables in great abundance. This extends, of course, to the luxury hotels; I've never seen a seafood bar like the one in the Siam Intercontinental! Live seafood cooked to order and to perfection. And in Singapore the whole thing was more or less underlined for me by a most impressive Chinese lady with whom I had a memorable long lunch. When I commented on her choice of a beautifully poached whole fish for our entree, she said, 'But of course! We Chinese have always lived this

23

way! We know we are what we put in our bodies, and we know our bodies change daily.'

Let me emphasize again that this book does not purport to be a cure for arthritis! Just about everyone has arthritis at some time or another; all this book purports to tell you is how to live.

EXERCISE

We all know that the body needs exercise in order to function properly. A moderate amount of sensible exercise will also help you to utilize these valuable foods; the improved circulation will aid in ridding your body of poisons.

I think it's safe to say that *everyone* has the basic exercise of walking available to him. No matter where or how you live, you can somehow get out and walk. The distance and pace depends on you and your condition; the important thing is to make it part of your daily routine, no matter how much you'd rather do something sedentary when you have the time. Swimming is probably considered to be the best exercise there is for any sort of arthritis. The body, being suspended in the water, is relieved of pressures and jolts, and yet the joints are being exercised. By all means take advantage of every opportunity to swim – even if it means going to public swimming baths in winter. (Actually, the indoor heated pools are better for you than chilly outdoor swimming.)

My favourite exercise, both for conditioning and pleasure, is bicycling. This is a sport that's gained tremendous popularity in recent years – ten years ago, when I took to riding on the streets of San Francisco, my teen-age daughter was mortified; now everyone is doing it. Some lucky communities have installed bike paths, but in almost all places there are parks and country roads to ride on. It takes no skill – we all learned as children, and bicycling is one of those things one never forgets.

Gardening can be good exercise, too, if you don't have to crouch or kneel in one position too long, particularly on the damp ground.

2

The Working Elements

In the complicated machinery of your body are all sorts of checks and balances. Vitamins and minerals are vitally important to you; all are present in the many vegetables you'll be eating. In most cases it is not necessary to add supplemental vitamins and minerals, but if you feel you need them, consult your doctor.

Actually, the primary concept of this regime is to consume only the basic, necessary foods instead of loading the body with extras it can't handle. The Western world is simply eating too much!

Protein is, of course, the first thing to be considered when choosing your foods. It is universally agreed that it's of utmost importance to maintenance of the body, formation of new tissues and cells, and resistance to disease. Since arthritis is a degenerative disease, I thought it wise to materially increase my daily intake of protein.

Seafood is a complete protein, completely digestible, and supplies in addition those valuable elements from the sea not available elsewhere. Of course, fresh fish is not possible for many because of geographical location, but there's always frozen fish and shellfish. Please, just read the label to be sure nothing has been added in the processing.

Of the vegetables; potatoes, cabbage, green peppers, and all the leafy greens are rich in the vitamins and minerals valuable to the arthritic. Brussels sprouts, beetroots, peas, beans, carrots, and celery are all very good. Make salads with raw vegetables as well as lettuce, since cooking may destroy their vitamins; serve them with shrimp, crab, or tuna and you have a complete lunch.

26

Sufferers from gout, a disease related to arthritis, must find out which of the vegetables listed on page 31 are to be avoided. Here common sense must enter in; everyone's body is different, and one must discover one's own anathemas by experimentation. For instance, some people might be allergic to nuts, but not all kinds of nuts. By the same token, some might be allergic to certain kinds of honey, depending on the flower from which the bee fed.

Unless you have 20–20 pluperfect vision, take your glasses with you to the grocery store. The law says that the ingredients must be listed on the label, but the size of the print is apparently not regimented. Try to buy products that have the purest ingredients; I cannot emphasize enough the importance of being a label reader. It is vital to avoid all additives and preservatives; one of your worst enemies is the chemical monosodium glutamate. The smallest amount of it can bring me days of discomfort.

Find a corn-oil margarine that is free of milk solids, and for salads mix corn oil with olive oil for flavour. I use both margarine and oil in cooking, and in very generous quantities; there is evidence that the presence of polyunsaturated fat is a factor in the strengthening of new cell membranes.

Dr Hugh M. Sinclair of the Department of Nutrition at Oxford University, vice-president of Oxford's Magdalen College and one of the world's foremost authorities on nutrition, has discovered some interesting facts. His discoveries, based on research, indicate that many of the so-called diseases of modern civilization are apparently the end result of a strange food deficiency. The missing substances are vitamin-like compounds known as essential unsaturated fatty acids, or UFA, found primarily in corn, peanut, cottonseed, and other vegetable oils. He indicates that a UFA deficiency seems to underlie certain conditions such as arthritis, allergy, bronchial asthma, skin diseases, and ulcerative colitis, as well as heart disease. The UFA chemicals, which seem to work somewhat like vitamins, include one potent substance known chemically as linoleic acid and

27

an even more potent compound called arachidonic acid. These chemicals, found in natural vegetable oils, are extremely sensitive to oxidation and are destroyed in the bleaching of flour, the frying of foods, and the hardening of natural oils that occurs in the manufacture of margarine.

If you inspect the label on a bottle of safflower oil, you will discover an interesting table of ratios between poly-unsaturated and saturated fats. Safflower oil has a ratio of 9 to 1, corn oil 5·3 to 1, soya bean oil 3·9 to 1, and cottonseed oil 2 to 1. Obviously these figures on the label, derived from a 1959 report of the U.S. Department of Agriculture, should not be ignored.

Whenever I find myself in the kitchen with a little time on my hands, I make a supply of frequently used items. Onions, garlic, and parsley are invaluable in this sort of cookery, and I chop onions and parsley and store them in jars with tight tops in the refrigerator. All my old chunks of leftover French bread go in the blender for breadcrumbs and are also stored in a jar.

Other acceptable seasonings, in addition to the parsley and onions just mentioned, are garlic, bay leaf, salt, and soya sauce. Please note that pepper is at no time mentioned. It is most definitely out, and the sooner you lose your taste for it the better. Incidentally, I was never so happy as when I discovered how to peel garlic without touching it. You simply give it a good whack with the flat side of your big knife or cleaver and the skin simply parts from the clove. Certain seasonings, such as the above and soya sauce, may be used indiscriminately; spices should be used very sparingly, very rarely, if at all – substitute herbs. However, in the beginning keep your entire diet pure and simple – you can launch into variations on the theme next year!

Chances are you'll remain more or less on this regime for the rest of your life, as I certainly intend to. Therefore, common sense is of the utmost importance. You wouldn't be doing this if you weren't troubled by arthritis to some degree; if you're in terrible shape you'll obviously follow the

28

diet to the letter, eschewing everything that is the least bit harmful. On the other hand, for some who feel remarkably better in a year or so it would seem reasonable to occasionally add a few goodies – things like a little dash of sherry in a sauce and a pinch of curry powder in a soup. Chicken broth, which I use throughout the book as a stock for soups and cooking, should not be used in the very beginning but may be added occasionally later. I now use it quite often with absolutely no ill effect. The same holds true for the white meat of chicken. I had been on the regime for a year and a half before I added, again occasionally, the white meat of chicken breasts. And did it taste good!

Flour of any kind is acceptable. However, very often I substitute cornflour. And I use arrowroot if I want a clear glaze-like sauce.

Sugar is, of course, perfectly acceptable, though fattening! Honey is a fine food, and the perfect substitute for preserves.

Remember that it's only the yolk of the egg you must eschew; egg whites are not only acceptable (the only acceptable dairy product), but a fine source of protein. With a little practice you can make a nice omelette from the white alone. It's possible, however, to make a quite acceptable substitute for the yolk of an egg. Take one large tablespoonful of soya bean flour, mix it with half a cup of water. Boil till it thickens, stirring constantly, and strain into a bowl. Beat in soya bean oil gradually until it's very thick, and add a pinch of salt. You can use this wherever you'd need the yolk of an egg, since it has much the same properties and flavour.

You can also make your own soya milk, and use it either for drinking (if you find the beany flavour palatable) or for cooking. Simply soak a cup of soya beans overnight, drain them, and grind them up in the blender. Add $4\frac{1}{2}$ pts of water, simmer for about half an hour, and drain out the solids through cheesecloth.

Remember, just about any idiot can be a good cook using

29

masses of butter and thick cream. And spicy seasonings can cover an army of cooking sins. There's real challenge in producing tempting, tasty fare while at the same time maintaining a rigid diet.

In general the recipes given in this book will serve from four to six, but the basic number of servings should be quite clear in every recipe. Only you will know about your appetite and that of your guests; by the same token, only you will know if one piece of a certain fish will serve one or two.

The first hurdle is one of attitude, isn't it? Habit is so strong, and at first you miss those old familiar foods. There will be a few days of feeling somewhat deprived; then wellbeing begins to take over and suddenly you decide it's all eminently worthwhile.

DO'S AND DON'TS

DO EAT

All seafoods
All vegetables, including avocados
Vegetable oils, particularly safflower and corn
Margarine free of milk solids
Egg whites
Honey
Nuts, sunflower seeds, soya bean products
Rice of all kinds: brown, white, wild
Bread to which nothing listed under 'DO NOT EAT' has been added
Tea and coffee
Plain soda water
Parsley, onions, garlic, bay leaf, salt
Any kind of flour
Sugar

DO NOT EAT

Meat in any form, including broth
Fruit of any kind, including tomatoes
Dairy products, including egg yolks, milk, cheese, yogurt
Vinegar, or any other acid
Pepper (definitely)
Chocolate
Dry roasted nuts (the process involves monosodium gluta-
    mate)
Alcoholic beverages
Soft drinks (I have never found one without additives)
All additives, preservatives, chemicals, most especially
    monosodium glutamate. One exception to this rule is
    the lecithin in margarine.

PERHAPS OCCASIONALLY

Breast of chicken and chicken broth
A small amount of wine in cooking
A small drink of whisky
A small pinch of spicy seasoning such as curry powder
Noodles or spaghetti, since the amount of egg is relatively
    small and somewhat broken down in the cooking

EXCEPTIONS

Persons who have gout, or who have been diagnosed as
having what is called gouty arthritis, will do well to avoid
certain things. This sensitivity must be determined by the
individual, since it varies from person to person, but in
general mushrooms, asparagus, spinach, artichokes, peas,
and beans are possible offenders. As for alcohol, whisky
does not seem to be right for some people with gout; I would
suggest vodka for their rare indulgence.

NOTES ON THE RECIPES IN THIS BOOK

Albacore tuna, which is available in the UK, is preferable to plain tuna (because of the mercury content) and should be used in the relevant recipes.

Fresh clams are not easily available in the UK, although tins of minced clams can be bought. However, most other types of shellfish can be substituted where clams are used in the following recipes – and equally court bouillon (fish stock) can be used instead of clam juice. Be sure there is no monosodium glutamate in the finised clams.

You may have some problems finding the ready-made Safflower Oil Mayonnaise which is used throughout the recipes so the following combination can be used as a substitute.

2 *tablespoons soya flour*
6 *tablespoons water*
½ *pt safflower oil* (*or some other type of polyunsaturated salad oil*)

Blend the soya flour and water to a paste. Add the oil, slowly at first (drop by drop), gradually increasing the flow to a teaspoon at a time until the mayonnaise starts to thicken, then add the oil at a faster rate, whisking throughout the whole process.

3
Appetizers

These are things to serve with those cocktails you don't drink but your friends most probably do. There are times when you want to have people in for something less than dinner, and some of these will serve the purpose. I always have a tray of raw vegetables for the many friends who are watching the calories, and I like to serve one hot canapé. (It looks as if you tried a little harder!)

CRUDITÉS

Cauliflower, broken into flowerettes
Carrot sticks
Green-pepper slices
Radishes, peeled back to flowers
Green onions
Small, fresh, raw, button mushrooms

Soak the raw vegetables in salted water in the refrigerator, and arrange in mounds on a large serving dish, with a dip in the centre of safflower oil mayonnaise mixed with soya sauce and some chopped chives and parsley.

GUACAMOLE

1 *large, very ripe avocado*
$\frac{1}{4}$ *teaspoon salt*
3 *teaspoons minced or grated onion*

Mix well and serve with tortillas or the raw vegetables listed in the previous recipe.

PIROSHKI

These delicious little Russian turnovers are quite sensational, and well worth the trouble of doing the pastry.

Filling:

1 *oz minced onion*
1 *oz margarine*
4 *oz chopped, cooked fish*
¼ *teaspoon crushed dill seed*
2 *tablespoons minced parsley*

Sauté the onion in the margarine, add the other ingredients, and if the mixture seems too dry add a little water. Place it in the centre of the following pastry, and fold over and patiently press the edges together until you're sure they'll stay.

Pastry:

½ *lb flour*
1 *teaspoon salt*
6 *oz margarine*
8 *tablespoons water*

Roll out thin and cut in 3-inch rounds; put in your filling; dampen the edges and press together firmly. Brush lightly with melted margarine and bake in a 400-degree oven until nicely browned.

SHRIMP PUFFS

3 *oz chopped, cooked shrimps*
1 *egg white, stiffly beaten*
¼ *pt safflower oil mayonnaise*
¼ *teaspoon salt*

Fold the egg white into the ingredients; pile the mixture on to thin slices of French bread, toasted; put under the grill until puffed and browned.

ARTICHOKE LEAVES WITH SHRIMP

Cook a nice large artichoke, separate the leaves, and arrange on each leaf a few small, cooked shrimps which have been moistened with a little safflower oil mayonnaise.

ARTICHOKE BOTTOMS

Fill artichoke bottoms with small shrimps mixed with safflower oil mayonnaise, or with crab legs. Olympia oysters are wonderful to use this way if you can get them. Minced clams mixed with a little diced celery and moistened with mayonnaise are also good.

AUBERGINE CAVIAR

1 *baked aubergine, pared, seeded, and mashed*
1 *green pepper, seeded and chopped*
1 *onion, chopped*
1 *clove of garlic, crushed*
3 *tablespoons olive oil*

Sauté the pepper and onion in the olive oil; add the garlic and aubergine. Salt to taste, and serve cold with crisp, thin wedges of toasted French bread.

35

SCALLOP PUFFS

1 *lb sea scallops*
3 *tablespoons safflower oil mayonnaise*
1 *tablespoon minced parsley*
½ *teaspoon soya sauce*
1 *egg white, stiffly beaten*

Simmer the scallops in about ½ pt of water in a covered pan for just a few minutes. Drain, cool, and cut in halves. Mix the mayonnaise with the parsley and soya sauce; beat the egg white and fold it in. Place the scallop halves on a baking sheet, top each with some of the mixture and brown under the grill.

GARLIC OLIVES

Drain the juice from a can of large, black olives. Put them in a jar with 3 cloves crushed garlic, cover them with olive oil, and let them stand several days. Green olives are good prepared this way too, but first crush them slightly. Black olives served hot are a pleasant surprise.

SWEET ALMONDS

These are delicious when roasted in a slow oven till brown and served hot.

4
Soups

I have found soups to be a very important part of my menu. The very form lends itself so admirably to the use of vegetables; the quantities and varieties are practically infinite.

First, it's imperative that you own a blender. If you've never had one, you'll find that experimentation with it opens a whole new field in cooking. You'll never wonder what to do with leftovers again!

Second, try to keep on hand a supply of chicken stock (to be used cautiously) and of court bouillon (see page 52) – homemade, because all tinned varieties that I know of have harmful additives. Read that label! For some soups I use clam juice, and for some the water the vegetables were cooked in. I keep a jar of vegetable water in my refrigerator; and sometimes a combination of, say, the water peas were cooked in and the water beetroots were cooked in will produce an unusual and interesting flavour.

When choosing a soup bear in mind the vegetables that are particularly high in the vitamins and minerals suspected to relieve arthritis. Green vegetables, particularly cabbage, and potatoes will make a rich, healthy soup for you. Potatoes are good to use as thickener for a creamy-type soup. Onions are also beneficial, as is garlic. And then of course there are all the seafood soups ... delicious, hearty, full of protein and all those natural minerals and vitamins from the sea that we have not as yet been able to ruin.

When you peer in the refrigerator and find leftover vegetables, rice, or potatoes, you have a soup started. All you need to do is put them in the blender with stock or water and add a few herbs or garlic salt. For instance, the other day I wanted a soup for lunch in cool weather. Checking the refrigerator, I turned up some leftover peas and a jar of chicken stock left from poaching some chicken breasts the night before. (This makes a lovely rich stock.)

I boiled a potato with a bunch of spring onions, squeezed in a clove of garlic, put it through the blender, and added the stock. Just before serving I added some frozen shrimp. It was delicious, a real 'homemade' soup, but I'd just made it up as I went along, adding and tasting. I've found you really can't go very far wrong when the ingredients are good, natural, and fresh to start with.

So experiment! Cook extra beetroots so you'll have some left over for borscht, use that extra rice as a thickener, and if you happen to be lucky enough to have leftover wild rice just stir it into a soup after it's been blended. Leftover fish can be used if it's been poached and filleted. In this case your stock would be either the court bouillon you have on hand or clam juice from a tin if you can obtain it.

CREAMY OYSTER SOUP

2 *oz diced celery*
1 *clove garlic, crushed*
1 *bunch chopped spring onions*
1 *potato, diced*
½ *pt fish stock*
1 *tin (about* 10 *oz) small oysters*
Parsley, chopped

Simmer the vegetables in the fish stock until very tender. Put through the blender, salt to taste, and add more stock if too thick. Add the oysters, heat, and serve immediately, sprinkled with the parsley.

LEEK AND POTATO SOUP

1 *bunch leeks, cut up (white part only)*
2 *medium potatoes, diced*
2 *pts water*
Salt
Tiny dash nutmeg
Chives, chopped

Sauté the leeks in margarine, add the other ingredients except the chives, and simmer till tender. Season, put through the blender, and serve sprinkled with the chives. Delicious cold, a mock vichyssoise.

FRESH PEA SOUP

Two 10-oz packets frozen peas (or equivalent amount of fresh)
2 *or 3 medium potatoes, diced*
2 *large onions, coarsely chopped*
Fat pinch sugar
Fat pinch salt
Pinch nutmeg

Cook the peas as directed on the packet, adding a fat pinch of sugar as well as salt. Boil the onions and potatoes in water to cover, and when tender combine with the peas and a small amount of margarine in the blender. Thin with water as necessary, and season with salt and a pinch of nutmeg.

GARLIC SOUP
(Wonderful for colds and 'flu)

1 *large head garlic, very fresh*
4 *pts chicken broth*

2 *pts water*
2 *cloves*
½ *bay leaf, pinch sage and thyme*
4 *sprigs parsley*
¾ *lb diced potatoes*
Handful stuffed green olives
3 *tablespoons olive oil*

Separate the garlic cloves and peel by laying on a cutting board and slapping hard with the flat side of a large-bladed knife or cleaver. The skin will fall away. Combine the garlic, water, cloves, herbs, and olive oil; simmer in the chicken broth, covered, 30 minutes. Add the potatoes and simmer another 20 minutes. Put through the blender, reheat, and serve with olives sliced on top.

Variation: Leave out the potatoes but simmer the additional time and pour over a thick slice of toasted French bread in each bowl.

MUSHROOM SOUP

½ *lb mushrooms, finely chopped*
1 *small onion, finely chopped*
Heaped teaspoon flour
1½ *pts water*
1 *oz margarine*

Sauté the mushrooms and onion in the margarine, blend in the flour, and add the water. Simmer about 10 minutes.

CRAB BISQUE

2 *oz frozen lima beans*
2 *oz sliced marrow*
2 *stalks celery, scraped and sliced*

2 oz crab meat, cooked or tinned
Dash paprika

Cover the vegetables with water and simmer till tender. Add the crab meat and put through the blender. Sprinkle with the paprika; reheat.

CHINESE CABBAGE SOUP

2 carrots, chopped
Small bunch parsley, minced
1 onion, finely chopped
½ head cabbage, finely chopped
2 oz margarine
Salt
2 pts water
Soya sauce

Sauté the vegetables in the margarine till tender; add water and simmer 30 minutes. Just before serving add soya sauce to taste.

BROWN BEAN SOUP

A 1-lb packet kidney beans
2 pts water
A ½-lb packet soup greens

Sauté the soup vegetables in margarine, boil the beans in the water according to the directions on the package (about 1½ hours), put everything through the blender, and salt to taste.

FAKE BONGO BONGO SOUP

1 *jar (about* 10 *oz) oysters, fresh*
3 *oz frozen spinach*
Tiny dash Worcestershire Sauce
Garlic salt to taste

Cook the spinach in ½ pt water till tender, add all the other ingredients, and put through the blender. Pour into oven-proof cups and top with a small drift of beaten egg white; put under the grill till browned.

BOUILLABAISSE

This wonderful Mediterranean feast can be made from many different assortments of fish and shellfish. It more or less depends on what is available to you. Haddock, halibut, sea bass, whiting, perch, trout, flounder, are all suitable for the fish part, and must be fresh, while the clams, scallops, crab, lobster, shrimp, and mussels can be fresh (preferably, of course) or frozen. The following version will give you an idea of the proportions.

2 *pounds haddock, halibut, sea bass, etc.*
2 *pts water*
½ *pt olive oil*
Thyme
Bay leaf
Fennel
2 *tablespoons minced parsley*
2 *onions, chopped*
1 *clove garlic, crushed*
½ *green pepper, seeded and chopped*
8 *oysters*
8 *mussels*

42

8 *clams*
6 *oz crab meat*
6 *oz lobster meat*
6 *oz shelled shrimp*
3 *oz sliced pimentos* (*or green peppers*)
Tiny pinch saffron

Boil the cleaned fish in the water until the water is reduced by half; save the broth; cut the fish into serving pieces. Place the olive oil in a heavy soup pot with the onions, garlic, pepper, and herbs; add the broth and boil rapidly 5 minutes. Add the boiled fish and simmer about an hour; add the rest of the seafood and the pimentos, and simmer another 10 minutes. Crumble the saffron into the soup and stir gently to distribute. Serve with crusty garlic French bread.

MEDITERRANEAN VEGETABLE SOUP

3 *or* 4 *potatoes, diced*
1 *lb fresh green beans, trimmed*
$\frac{1}{2}$ *lb spaghetti*
3 *cloves garlic*
3 *tablespoons olive oil*
Small handful fresh basil leaves, or heaped tablespoon dried
Cook the vegetables in 3 pts water, salted well. When they are almost tender, break the spaghetti into the pot and finish cooking very slowly. Grind the basil, garlic, and oil in a mortar and pestle and mix into the soup.

VEGETABLE SOUP

1 *leek, scrubbed and sliced thin*
1 *medium onion, cubed*

1 *small, white turnip, cubed*
2 *carrots, diced*
2 *oz sliced celery*
1 *oz chopped parsley*
1½ *oz margarine*
3 *potatoes, cubed*
1½ *teaspoons salt*

Place all the ingredients except the potatoes and salt in a pot; cook, stirring, 3 or 4 minutes. Then add the potatoes and salt and about 4 pts water; cook about 1 hour, or until the vegetables are tender. Serve with a sprinkle of minced parsley.

WATERCRESS SOUP

Put a large, bunch of fresh watercress, stems and all, in a pot with a cut-up potato and a bunch of sliced leeks. Add about 2 pts of water; salt well and simmer till the potato is tender. Put through the blender a very few seconds, just enough to chop the watercress but not enough to purée.

GARDEN SOUP

This is a more elaborate soup using watercress. It uses many of the same ingredients as my other soups, but this particular combination produces a uniquely elegant and delicate soup to serve, for instance, before a rather elaborate dinner.

1 *bunch watercress*
½ *head crisp round lettuce*
4 *spring onions, all of them*
4 *outside cabbage leaves*
Bunch parsley

44

Sprig fresh thyme, if possible (or substitute pinch of powdered)
2 pts chicken broth
Salt
Margarine

Chop the vegetables fine; sauté, stirring, in margarine about 10 minutes. Add the broth; cover and simmer 30 minutes. Season with salt, and put through the blender; reheat.

OLD-FASHIONED PEA SOUP

Start soaking 1 cup dried peas about 10.30 A.M. At 3.00 P.M. put them on to boil covered with a liberal supply of water. About 5.00 P.M. add a potato, finely diced, and a chopped onion. Add water when needed. Put the soup in a double boiler for one more hour.

SCALLOP CHOWDER

This is one of the few chowder recipes that taste like chowder without the inclusion of all the *verboten* ingredients like bacon or pork.

1 lb sea scallops
1½ oz margarine
1 medium onion, chopped
3 stalks celery, sliced
2 pts boiling water
¼ green pepper, chopped
6 medium sweet potatoes, peeled and sliced in 1-inch pieces
1 pt court bouillon
2 teaspoons salt
2 teaspoons cornflour

Sauté the onion and celery in the margarine; add the boiling water, green pepper, potatoes, fish stock, and salt. Cook over

45

medium heat 15 minutes; add the scallops and cook 10 minutes longer. Check the potatoes for tenderness; lastly stir in the cornflour (which has been mixed with a little cold water).

AVOCADO BISQUE

1 *large, ripe avocado*
1 *tablespoon minced onion*
½ *oz margarine*
1 *tablespoon flour*
1 *pt chicken stock*

Sauté the minced onion slowly in some margarine. Make a *roux* of the flour and the tablespoon of margarine and add the chicken stock gradually. Press the avocado through a sieve; add it to the onion and stir quickly for about half a minute. Add the stock and salt to taste. Serve hot with croutons.

JELLIED BORSCHT

1 *pt beetroot juice (made from boiling about 4 beetroots in 2 pts water)*
1½ *pts fish stock*
3 *whole cloves*
1 *medium onion, chopped*
2 *cabbage leaves*
1 *tablespoon unflavoured gelatine in 2 tablespoons cold water*

Combine the beetroot juice and stock with the cloves, onion, and cabbage leaves; simmer 10 minutes. Strain, and to the liquid add the gelatine mixed with water. This will make a thin jelly, and if you wish it thicker add more gelatine. Chill and serve sprinkled with a few dill seeds.

46

VICHYSSOISE

1 *large potato*
1 *oz margarine*
1 *medium onion, chopped*
2 *pts chicken broth*
Dash nutmeg
Salt
Chives, finely chopped

Cut the potato in cubes, simmer in the broth till cooked.
Meanwhile sauté the onion in the margarine, being careful
not to brown it; cover it with a lid and let it stand till the
potato is done. Purée all together in the blender with the
nutmeg and salt, chill for several hours, and serve topped
with the chives. (This is quite a thick soup; if it seems too
thick, thin it with a little water.)

COLD CUCUMBER SOUP

1 *very large or* 2 *small cucumbers*
½ *pt fish stock*
Pinch curry powder

Peel and dice the cucumber and put everything in the
blender. Purée and serve very cold.

CLAM BROTH WITH DICED AVOCADO

Combine ½ pt of clam juice with 1 pt chicken broth, and
serve with diced avocado floating in it.

CLAM BROTH WITH CELERY

Make a celery broth from the leaves of celery, add an equal part of clam juice, and serve with finely chopped celery in it.

OYSTER STEW

¾ *lb frozen oysters or substitute 2 quarts mussels*
2 *oz margarine*
3 *oz finely chopped celery*
1½ *pts chicken stock*
Parsley or chervil, chopped
Salt to taste

Cook the oysters and celery in the margarine about 3 minutes. Add the chicken stock, and when hot salt to taste and serve sprinkled with the chervil or parsley.

CREAM OF ONION SOUP

3 *large, sweet Spanish onions, sliced thin*
1 *pt clam juice or chicken broth*
½ *pt water*
2 *medium potatoes, sliced*
1 *oz margarine*
4 *oz chopped Spanish onion*
1 *tablespoon cornflour*
1 *teaspoon salt*
Parsley, chopped

Cook the onion slices in the liquid 20 minutes. If you prefer, you may substitute chicken broth for the clam juice. I must remind you here that the chicken broth you use is an occasional goody, not something for the daily menu. Add the potatoes and salt and cook 15 minutes longer; purée in the blender. Sauté the chopped onion in the margarine until golden; blend in the cornflour, which has been mixed with a little cold water; add this to the puréed mixture and bring to a boil, thinning with clam juice if too thick. Sprinkle on the chopped parsley before serving.

ONION SOUP

1½ oz margarine
¾ lb chopped onion
½ oz flour
3 pts water
1 bay leaf
Salt to taste
French bread

Sauté the onion in the margarine till browned; blend in the flour. Stir in the water gradually, add the bay leaf and salt, and cook over low heat 30 minutes. Discard the bay leaf. Place a slice of toasted French bread in each bowl and pour the soup over it.

FRENCH SEAFOOD BISQUE

This is a divine rich mixture of seafood. It makes a wonderful winter luncheon dish.

2½ oz margarine
2 tablespoons each minced parsley, onion, carrot, celery
½ lb cooked crab or lobster meat (fresh, frozen, or tinned), coarsely chopped
½ lb cooked shrimp, coarsely chopped
A ½-lb tin minced clams or fresh shellfish of choice

1½ *pts clam juice or fish stock*
3 *tablespoons dry white wine* (*it adds so much to this soup, and the harm is almost cooked out*)
½ *teaspoon thyme*
2 *tablespoons cornflour*
Salt
Pinch nutmeg

Sauté the minced vegetables in 1 oz of the margarine until soft. Add the crab, shrimp, clams, liquid, and thyme. Heat about 5 minutes without allowing to boil. Make a *roux* of the remaining 1½ oz of margarine and the cornflour (which has been mixed with a little cold water), and gradually add the liquid from the seafood pan. Stir until thickened, and season with salt and nutmeg. Put about half the seafood mixture in the blender for just a few seconds; then combine all the ingredients and reheat before serving.

CREAM OF ALMOND SOUP

4 *oz blanched almonds*
2 *pts chicken broth*
Bouquet of 3 *sprigs parsley*, 2 *sprigs thyme*, 1 *piece celery, all tied together, and* 1 *chopped onion*
1 *oz margarine*
2 *tablespoons cornflour*

Grate the almonds in the blender; combine them with the broth, bouquet, and onion in a pan; simmer 30 minutes. Discard the bouquet. In another pan melt the margarine; stir in the cornflour mixed with a little water; add a little of the soup mixture till thickened; then put everything together; boil and stir 1 minute; and taste for seasoning. Garnish with toasted, slivered almonds.

PEASANT VEGETABLE SOUP

2 *carrots, scraped and sliced*
3 *leeks, thinly sliced*
1 *parsnip, peeled and thinly sliced*
½ *lb chopped cabbage*
1½ *oz margarine*
4 *pts water*
1 *bay leaf*
A 10- *or* 12-*oz packet frozen mixed vegetables*
2 *oz rice*
6 *oz chopped spinach*
6 *oz chopped lettuce*

Sauté the carrots, leeks, parsnip, and cabbage in the margarine. Add the water, bay leaf, mixed vegetables, and rice. Cook covered over low heat 20 minutes or until the rice is done; discard the bay leaf, then add the spinach and lettuce and cook 5 minutes. Salt to taste.

GREENS SOUP

2 *oz chopped shallots*
2 *oz margarine*
8 *oz diced potatoes*
2 *pts water*
4 *oz watercress*
4 *oz chopped lettuce*
4 *oz spinach or sorrel*

Sauté the shallots in margarine 5 minutes. Add the potatoes, water, watercress, lettuce, and spinach. Cover and cook 15 minutes over low heat. Put through the blender and stir in a dollop of margarine; salt to taste.

51

NEW ORLEANS GUMBO

½ *lb shrimps*
2 *pts water*
½ *oz margarine*
1 *small onion, minced*
1 *clove garlic, minced*
1 *stalk celery, chopped*
1 *bay leaf*
2 *sprigs parsley, chopped*
½ *teaspoon thyme*
1 *tablespoon cornflour*
3 *tablespoons water*
½ *pint oysters*

Shell the shrimps. Boil the shells 10 minutes; discard the shells; add water to make 2 pts. Brown the onion, garlic, celery, bay leaf, parsley, and thyme in the margarine. Add them to the stock, thicken with cornflour softened in water, and boil 1 hour. Add the shrimps and oysters, cooking gently till the oysters curl.

COURT BOUILLON

You will need this stock for many recipes in this book. You can make it ahead and keep it in a jar in the refrigerator for up to a week.

2 *lb fish trimmings*
4 *pts water*
1 *bay leaf*
¼ *lb margarine*
2 *carrots, sliced*
3 *stalks celery, chopped*
1 *large onion, sliced*

Pinch thyme
3 *sprigs parsley*
2 *teaspoons salt*

Boil everything together for 1 hour; strain.

VEGETABLE SOUP PROVENÇAL

1 *lb courgettes*
½ *teaspoon salt*
6½ *oz chopped onion*
1 *clove garlic*
1 *lb fresh lima beans*
3 *pts water*
8 *oz fresh peas*

Pistou:

4 *cloves garlic*
Handful parsley
Handful basil
2 *tablespoons olive oil mixed with safflower oil*
¼ *pt safflower oil mayonnaise*

Grate the courgettes and add the salt; let set awhile, then put through the blender, with the juice. Sauté the onions and 1 clove garlic in margarine till translucent but not browned; add the courgettes and sauté a few more minutes. Now add the lima beans to the water; boil till almost done and add the peas. Put through the blender and add to the courgette-onion mixture.

Serve topped with a large spoonful of this version of *pistou*: Crush 4 cloves garlic in a pestle with the parsley and basil. Add the oil to the mixture as you grind, and when smooth add the mayonnaise. Serve this soup with some nice homemade French bread!

MINESTRONE

¼ *lb butter beans*
½ *lb courgettes*
1 *medium potato*
¾ *lb cabbage, cut in small strips*
¼ *lb green string beans, cut in small pieces*
4 *pts water*
2 *tablespoons olive oil*
1 *oz chopped onions*
1 *clove garlic, crushed*
2 *oz rice*
3 *tablespoons chopped parsley*
Salt and basil to taste

Pour boiling water over the butter beans and let stand 2 hours. Drain. Put them in the 4 pts water and cook 1 hour. Sauté the onions in the oil; peel and dice the potato and courgettes, add them to the onion mixture, and sauté 5 more minutes. Add them to the butter beans; then add the green beans, cabbage, garlic, salt, and basil. Cover and cook over low heat 1¼ hours. Add the rice and chopped parsley and cook 20 minutes more, or until the rice is done.

CHICKEN VEGETABLE SOUP

4 *pts chicken stock*
½ *lb diced chicken breasts*
1 *teaspoon salt*
4 *oz diced celery*
2 *shallots, chopped*
1 *carrot, sliced*
1 *medium-sized onion, sliced*
3 *whole cloves*
½ *teaspoon nutmeg*

1 *tablespoon chopped parsley*
1 *bay leaf (fresh, if possible)*
½ *lb mixed vegetables of your choice (a nice combination is courgettes, mushrooms, and green beans)*
½ *lb cooked rice*

Add the diced chicken and the salt to the stock and bring to a boil. Skim the surface until no more fat rises. Allow to simmer 1 hour. Add the remaining ingredients. Bring to a boil and skim again. Simmer 2 hours. Serves 12.

5
Salads

As bread is my breakfast, so salad seems to have become my daily luncheon. And most important, I can always find a salad on a restaurant menu and know that the ingredients haven't been tampered with in the kitchen. I simply ask for an oil dressing – skip the vinegar, please! And I particularly like garlic salt, so I find an oil–garlic salt dressing very palatable.

Leftover cooked vegetables are delicious in salads. One can make all kinds of variations on, say, the Salade Niçoise by cleaning out the refrigerator. Tuna fish, the solid white albacore kind, is a mainstay, and Saffola or another safflower oil mayonnaise is delicious when mixed with a little soya sauce and a squeeze of garlic.

Another wonderful dressing is made with shallots – admittedly not always easy to get but well worth it for their subtle, gentle, oniony flavour tinged with garlic. Peel and slice them very thin, and add them to your oil with salt. This is a great dressing for raw or very slightly cooked vegetable salads. It's best if allowed to marinate a while before being served.

In preparing vegetables for salad, some such as courgettes and mushrooms should be sliced thinly and served raw; green beans, carrots, beetroots, and the like should be cooked till barely done and then sliced. Run cold water over them to cool immediately after cooking.

SALADE NIÇOISE

New potatoes, boiled whole
Green beans, cooked crisp
Beetroots, cooked or canned
Tuna, the best chunky white
Anchovies and black olives

Chill all the ingredients and arrange on a bed of lettuce in the desired proportions. Decorate with strips of anchovy and olives. Crush 1 clove garlic in ¼ pt olive oil, add a touch of dry mustard and lots of salt, and pour over salad.

ASPARAGUS SALAD

Another delicious salad plate, suitable for an entire luncheon, is based on fresh asparagus. Add shrimps (cooked, shelled, and deveined), artichoke hearts, and pitted ripe olives. Arrange them attractively on lettuce and serve with an oil dressing to which you've added (mixed *very* well) a crushed clove of garlic, ½ teaspoon cumin seed, a pinch of dry mustard, a pinch of paprika, and about ⅛ teaspoon salt.

CHINESE SALAD

1 *lb spinach*
3 *tablespoons oil*
½ *lb small shrimps*
2 *tablespoons soya sauce*

Cook the spinach; rinse in ice-cold water; chop. Combine the oil, soya sauce, and shrimps and add to the spinach. Serve very cold.

ENDIVE AND BEETROOT SALAD

Chop endive and cooked beetroots, toss together in oil, and salt to taste.

SARAH BERNHARDT SALAD

Line a salad bowl with leaves of lettuce and in the centre make a bed of shredded lettuce. Place a bunch of asparagus tips upright in the centre and surround it with artichoke bottoms and mounds of minced celery mixed with safflower oil mayonnaise. Pour over this a dressing made of olive oil seasoned with a little soya sauce and garlic salt.

RUSSIAN SALAD I

Place three artichoke bottoms on a bed of watercress; fill one with shrimp and diced celery, mixed with safflower oil mayonnaise; one with rolled anchovies sprinkled with chopped chives; and one with diced sardines, crab flakes, and caviar. Serve with olive oil and onion salt. This very fancy version makes a lovely first course for a dinner party or buffet.

RUSSIAN SALAD II

This is a delicious, healthy version in which you can use almost any combination of vegetables. Line a bowl with lettuce; place mounds of diced beetroots, potatoes, string beans, and peas around a small head of cauliflower in the centre. I like all the vegetables cooked *al dente*, crisp and chilled. Serve with safflower oil mayonnaise mixed with 3 tablespoons soya sauce.

AVOCADOS

We prefer to eat avocados the epicurean way. Simply cut the avocado in half, remove the stone and place it on a few lettuce leaves or a bed of watercress. Sprinkle the avocado with a few drops of oil and salt and eat it with a spoon.

CELERY-HEART SALAD

Celery hearts are only available at certain times of the year, but they are well worth the trouble of boiling till tender and peeling away all the dark outside. Dice the white part, mix with oil and garlic salt, and serve on watercress.

CUCUMBER AND WATERCRESS SALAD

This salad is made in the proportions of $\frac{1}{3}$ watercress to $\frac{2}{3}$ cucumbers cut in $\frac{1}{2}$-inch dice; it's a good combination served with oil and garlic salt or safflower oil mayonnaise.

CELERY-HEART AND AVOCADO SALAD

On a nest of lettuce arrange slices of avocado alternated with pieces of celery heart cut as nearly as possible the same size. Garnish with shredded beetroot and parsley, and serve with olive oil and salt.

MUSHROOM AND FENNEL SALAD

1½ *lb fresh mushrooms*
3 *fennel hearts or celery hearts*

¼ *pt safflower oil mayonnaise*
1 *tablespoon mustard*
3 *tablespoons oil*
Salt
Lettuce

Wipe the mushrooms after washing thoroughly. Chop them together with the fennel until very fine. Make a dressing of the other ingredients and serve on a bed of lettuce.

CUCUMBER AND MUSHROOM ASPIC

1 *pt water*
2 *bay leaves, crumbled*
2 *teaspoons tarragon*
Celery salt
2 *packets unflavoured gelatine, softened in a little cold water*
1 *teaspoon grated onion*
About ½ pt ice cubes and water
4 *oz peeled cucumber*
5 *oz sliced fresh mushrooms*
1 *oz pimento strips (or green peppers)*
Salad greens, cold and crisp

Bring to a boil the water, bay leaves, tarragon, and celery salt. Pour this over the gelatine; stir until dissolved. Let stand 5 minutes; strain; add onion, ice cubes, and water. Stir until the ice melts; chill till very thick. Peel and flute the cucumbers; stem the mushrooms; blot both with paper towels; then slice the mushrooms lengthwise. With the pimento, fold them into the gelatine. Chill in a pint mould and serve turned out on a chilled plate surrounded by crisp greens.

CLAM SALAD

This doesn't sound too terribly good, but it is. I invented it one day when I couldn't find anything but these ingredients for lunch.

½-lb tin chopped clams (not the minced variety)
Several stalks tender celery, diced
3 spring onions with a little of the green top
About ¼ green pepper, cut in slivers
Safflower oil mayonnaise
Lettuce

Drain the clams but not too thoroughly, so that you retain just a little of their juice. Mix all the ingredients together with just enough mayonnaise to hold it together and season to taste. Serve on a bed of crisp lettuce.

CALIFORNIA SALAD

4 oz sliced fresh mushrooms
4 oz cooked baby shrimps
1 teaspoon tarragon
About 5 tablespoons olive oil
Salt
Ripe chilled avocados
Crisp lettuce

Combine the mushrooms, shrimps, tarragon, and oil; salt generously. Chill in the refrigerator and serve in peeled, halved avocados on a bed of lettuce.

AIOLI

This is used in Provence in many ways, but I find it delicious with fresh cooked or raw vegetables. It can be served in a bowl with the vegetables surrounding it in separate dishes, or it can be used simply as an adjunct to the vegetable served with the main course.

6 *cloves garlic, peeled and crushed*
1 *cup safflower oil mayonnaise*
3 *tablespoons olive oil*
Salt

Add the garlic to the mayonnaise; add the oil little by little. Salt to taste.

MOULDED TUNA SALAD

1 *tablespoon unflavoured gelatine, softened in a little cold water*
3 *tablespoons cold fish stock*
3 *tablespoons hot chicken stock*
9 *tablespoons safflower oil mayonnaise*
4 *oz flaked albacore tuna*
2 *tablespoons chopped ripe olives*
1 *oz slivered, blanched almonds*
Chopped celery, walnuts, pimento to taste

Mix everything together and chill in a 9-inch ring mould for fish, or any other mould.

LOBSTER-TAIL SALAD

Lobster tails are so flavourful that they need little dressing up. Drop the frozen tails in salted boiling water with a bay leaf for about 5 minutes; drain and chill. Cut into salad-size pieces and marinate in olive oil, dill, and chopped parsley for several hours. Serve on crisp lettuce.

FISH SALAD

This is served at a Greek restaurant in London, the White Tower. It is served in variations all around the Mediterranean, and makes a perfect summer luncheon dish.

1 *lb firm white fish (such as turbot), poached, drained, and chilled*
1 *oz chopped onion*
1 *oz chopped parsley*
1 *large bay leaf, finely crumbled*
About 5 tablespoons olive oil
Salt
Celery root

Cut the fish into neat bite-sized cubes; marinate with dressing made from the other ingredients. Serve slivered celery root on the side.

CHICKEN SALAD

1 *lb diced, cooked chicken breasts*
¼ *lb diced celery*
4 *spring onions, including some tops, minced*
1 *teaspoon chopped dill or basil*
½ *pt safflower oil mayonnaise*
½ *cucumber, peeled and diced*

Mix everything together and serve very cold on crisp lettuce leaves.

COLESLAW

This is probably the most important of the salads. It just could not be better for you! Make it often! Shred raw cabbage and soak it in ice water in the refrigerator for an hour or so before using. Drain and dry carefully, blotting and turning in paper towels. Add lots of thinly sliced green pepper, grated onion, and, if desired, grated raw carrot. Add some dill weed if you like, lots of salt, and a small amount of salad oil. Bind everything together with safflower oil mayonnaise.

SCANDINAVIAN HERRING SALAD

2 *large salt herrings*
10 *oz diced, boiled potatoes*
8 *oz diced beetroot*
½ *onion, chopped*
2 *tablespoons oil*
¼ *pt safflower oil mayonnaise*
Crisp lettuce

Wash the herrings; cut off the heads and tails and soak in cold water overnight. Drain and fillet; dice the fillets, carefully removing any skin. Toss everything carefully so as not to break the potatoes and beetroot; chill thoroughly; serve on crisp lettuce.

GREEN SALAD WITH CROUTONS

With all the different sorts of lettuce available, there's no reason not to have lots of variety; with the addition of some sliced cucumbers and croutons you have a rather different green salad. For the croutons, make cubes of leftover French bread and sauté them in olive oil in which you have crushed a clove of garlic. It goes without saying, I hope, that you always dry your lettuce most carefully, patting each leaf if necessary. A French wire lettuce basket that you swing is great but requires a back-door area unless you don't mind a little rain in your kitchen.

64

SHRIMP SALAD WITH RICE AND PEAS

Here is a delicious salad, complete in all nutrients for a balanced meal.

Put the following in a heavy pan and simmer 30 minutes. (The bouquet garni should be in cheesecloth for easy removal.)

$\frac{1}{2}$ *pt olive oil*
$1\frac{1}{2}$ *pts water*
$\frac{1}{4}$ *pt soya sauce*
$\frac{1}{2}$ *teaspoon tabasco*
Salt
Bouquet garni composed of:
  2 leeks or 6 spring onions, cut in pieces
  1 teaspoon tarragon
  Bunch celery leaves
  Handful parsley
  3 cloves
  Small piece of cinnamon stick

Now add about 3 lb raw, peeled, and deveined shrimps and bring back to a boil. After about 10 seconds remove from the stove and let stand till cool. Refrigerate overnight. The following day remove the shrimps with a slotted spoon and boil the marinade down to about 1 pt. Remove *bouquet garni*. Add about 2 table-spoons cornflour very carefully (mixed with a little cold water first, of course) and then fold in 3 stiffly beaten egg whites.

Meanwhile you have cooked and drained 1 lb rice; while the rice is still warm mix in salt, a pinch of nutmeg, a bunch of finely chopped spring onions, and several tablespoons olive oil.

With your other hand you've put in a pan some margarine, about 2 tablespoons finely minced onion, and $\frac{1}{4}$ pt water. Cook until the water has boiled away and the onion is soft.

65

Stir in 1 packet frozen peas (over which hot water has been poured to defrost); mix well; and you're ready to serve. Mound the peas in the centre of a round platter, make a ring of rice around them, add a ring of shrimps around that, and decorate the edge with attractive lettuce leaves, watercress, or parsley. Serve the sauce separately.

CRAB LOUIS

This is another hearty lunch salad; use whatever crab you can get – fresh crab is preferable. Arrange the crab meat on a bed of crisp, cold lettuce and cover with the following dressing.

1 *pt safflower oil mayonnaise*
2 *oz finely chopped spring onions*
2 *oz finely chopped seeded green pepper*
3 *tablespoons soya sauce*
Salt to taste

AVOCADO MOUSSE

5 *mashed very ripe avocados*
2 *tablespoons unflavoured gelatine in ¼ pt cold water*
¼ *pt boiling water*
½ *teaspoon onion powder*
1 *teaspoon salt*
Dash tabasco
2 *tablespoons minced parsley*
¼ *pt safflower oil mayonnaise*

Soak the gelatine in cold water 5 minutes; dissolve in the boiling water. Put the avocado in the blender with the parsley and everything but the mayonnaise. Then fold in the

66

latter and pour the mixture into a quart mould which has been rinsed out with cold water. Chill till firm; serve mould on a bed of watercress.

GREEN GODDESS DRESSING

8 *anchovy fillets*
1 *spring onion*
Handful parsley
8–10 *leaves fresh tarragon, or 2 teaspoons dried*
1 *oz chives*
1½ *pts safflower oil mayonnaise*

Put everything in the blender and run till smooth. Serve cold over firm lettuce.

CAULIFLOWER SALAD

1 *lb cold, cooked cauliflower*
4 *spring onions, chopped*
1 *green pepper, seeded and chopped*
2 *anchovies, chopped*
2 *oz diced beetroots*
¼ *pt safflower oil mayonnaise*

Mix everything together and serve very cold on crisp lettuce leaves.

SALAD MIXTURES

Use your imagination with combinations like cold cauliflower, strips of green pepper, thinly sliced celery, spring onions, and diced avocado. A tin of chopped ripe olives is an interesting addition to a green salad. Broccoli and courgettes make a good combination served with oil and garlic salt.

CRAB-MEAT LUNCHEON PLATTER

Make a large bed of crisp lettuce in the centre of the platter. In this place a mound of crab meat mixed with chopped celery and safflower oil mayonnaise. Around the crab meat make a rim of frozen baby lima beans which have been cooked and chilled in a marinade of olive oil and onion salt.

JELLIED CRAB-MEAT SALAD

1 *tablespoon unflavoured gelatine, softened in a little cold water*
3 *tablespoons hot water*
9 *tablespoons safflower oil mayonnaise*
2 *oz diced celery*
2 *tablespoons chopped green olives*
$\frac{1}{2}$ *green pepper, minced*
$\frac{1}{2}$ *teaspoon salt*
6 *oz crab meat*
2 *tablespoons chopped pimentos (or green peppers)*

Soak the gelatine in the hot water 5 minutes. Add to the mayonnaise slowly; then immediately add the gelatine–mayonnaise mixture to all the other ingredients and chill in a ring mould.

CELERY VICTOR

Select uniform stalks of dwarf celery or hearts of celery. Wash, unseparated, and simmer in water and soya sauce (about 1 part sauce to 4 parts water) until tender. Drain carefully; marinate in olive oil, dill weed, and garlic salt for several hours before serving, chilled.

JELLIED CUCUMBER SALAD

3 *teaspoons unflavoured gelatine, softened in a little cold water*
½ *pt hot water*
4 *cucumbers, peeled and grated*
1 *tablespoon onion juice*
¼ *teaspoon salt*

Dissolve the softened gelatine in the hot water. When cool add the remaining ingredients and chill in a ring mould.

SCALLOPS IN CUCUMBERS

4–6 *long cucumbers*
2 *oz diced celery*
2 *pimentos (or green peppers), chopped fine*
½ *green pepper, chopped fine*
1 *lb scallops, cooked and diced*
2 *tablespoons safflower oil mayonnaise*
½ *small onion, grated*
Onion salt to taste

Peel the cucumbers and cut lengthwise; scoop out the seeds and chill. Combine the celery, pimentos and green pepper, scallops, mayonnaise, and onion. Add onion salt to taste. Fill the cucumbers with the mixture and serve on salad greens or watercress.

SCALLOP SALAD

2 *lb scallops*
4 *oz diced cucumber*
4 *oz thinly sliced celery*
1 *oz sliced, stuffed green olives*
½ *pt safflower oil mayonnaise*
A little oil to thin

Combine everything and serve on watercress.

ALMOND CUCUMBER SALAD

2 *cucumbers, peeled and sliced very thin*
½ *teaspoon salt*
½ *pt safflower oil mayonnaise*
1 *oz chopped, blanched, and toasted almonds*
2 *tablespoons minced chives*

Mix everything together, chill, and serve on a bed of crisp lettuce leaves.

OYSTER OR MUSSEL SALAD

2 *dozen oysters or 2 quarts mussels*
  Safflower oil mayonnaise to which has been added 1 finely chopped anchovy

Simmer oysters or mussels in their own liquid for a minute or two. Chill and serve coated with mayonnaise on a bed of lettuce.

HEARTS OF LETTUCE WITH AVOCADO DRESSING

2 *very ripe avocados*
1 *tablespoon grated onion*
Salt to taste

Put the avocado through a blender, mix with onion, salt to taste, and serve on chilled lettuce hearts.

CHEF'S SALAD BOWL

I have a plastic salad bowl with a cover that I keep in the freezer. I take the icy-cold bowl from the freezer, put a salad together, all but the dressing, and have it crisping in the refrigerator while I do other things. Don't put the dressing on till you're ready to serve, however. This is my Sunday luncheon salad.

1 *medium head Cos lettuce*
¼ *medium head round lettuce*
½ *bunch chicory*
¼ *bunch watercress*
½ *lb shredded cabbage*
4 *oz small shrimps*
4 *oz breast of chicken cut in thin strips*
1 *medium green pepper, cut in strips*
6 *green olives, chopped*
1 *bunch spring onions, finely chopped*

Break the greens into bite-size pieces; combine everything in a bowl, with the shrimps and chicken on top. When ready to serve pour over this a dressing of ½ pt safflower oil mayonnaise mixed with 3 tablespoons soya sauce and 2 cloves crushed garlic. Toss at the table.

71

SPINACH SALAD

1 *tablespoon chopped white onion*
2 *tablespoons diced celery*
1 *teaspoon sliced green pepper*
½ *teaspoon chopped fresh parsley*
1 *lb fresh, young spinach, washed and chilled*
3 *tablespoons olive oil*
¼ *teaspoon salt*
Pinch dry mustard
¼ *teaspoon oregano*

Mince the onion, celery, green pepper, and parsley together until very fine and pulpy. Add the oil and seasonings and let stand for quite a while to blend well. Pour this over the spinach leaves, which have been torn into small pieces, and toss.

6
Seafood

A glance at the globe will tell you that the earth is predominantly covered with water. Is it any wonder, then, that whole populations have been living on fish since time began? There have been whole populations of healthy, vital, fish-eating people all through history, particularly seafarers such as the Vikings. Even today fish constitutes the major source of food for people all over the world; the exception is the affluent United States. The United States has the highest arthritic rate in the world!

Fish is a perfect source of protein, low in fats, high in minerals and vitamins. All seafood contains a supply of iron, magnesium, iodine, calcium, copper, phosphorus, and fluorides.

However, you may ask, 'What about mercury pollution?' No one can be unaware of this subject. Mercury has been present in our seafood for thousands of years – probably, in fact, since the beginning of time – and admittedly the extreme toxicity of mercury has been recognized for over a thousand years, but recently dangerous industrial spillages have raised the question of safety.

Various opinions have been voiced, but I quote from some of our soundest experts. Dr Leonard J. Goldwater – Professor of Community Health Services at Duke University, Visiting Professor in Environmental Sciences at the University of North Carolina, Professor Emeritus of Occupational Medicine at Columbia University, consultant to various groups such as the World Health Organization, the Environmental Protection Agency, and the fishing, canning, paint and mercury industries – has some heartening things to say on the subject. His interest dates back to 1936, and he states that no case of mercury poisoning from seafood has ever been suspected in the United States or Canada; mercury poisoning has been limited to people who have existed on an unbalanced diet not intended for human consumption. Dr Goldwater criticizes the instant experts and the 'press-inspired hysteria over mercury in food fish' and says flatly that Americans can eat fish without fear of mercury poisoning. Dr Thomas B. Eyl of St Clair, Michigan, found no cases of mercury poisoning in a study of longtime heavy-to-moderate fish eaters whose fish came from a lake known to be polluted with mercury.

Published reports in recent years have found excess levels of mercury in some swordfish and tinned tuna; you won't find recipes for swordfish or large tuna in this book. It seems that the retention of mercury increases in direct relation to the size of the fish. An article in the *Saturday Review* for 6 February, 1971, states it this way:

> The danger of mercury poisoning in fish generally increases with the size of the fish. To provide an adequate number of marketable cuts, swordfish must run upwards of 100 pounds in weight. Therefore the chances are high that swordfish will remain off the market in this country because of the mercury threat. There is a greater chance that tuna supplies will be less curtailed for the following reasons. Tuna meat is classified by its colour, with the white meat of albacore the most popular, then the progressively darker meat of the yellow fin, the skipjack, the big eye, and the blue fin. Albacore average 45 pounds, yellow fin 150, big eye 235, blue fin even more.

Mercury has been used in medicine for centuries. Mercurial diuretics for kidney diseases are given in amounts many thousands of times greater than that found in fish, often with life-saving results. And incidentally, the mercury level in our cattle and other foodstuffs tends to make the seafood level look safer by comparison.

As to the availability of seafood, it's certainly easier if you're near one of our coasts ... but with the modern transportation and facilities for quick freezing, fish is really obtainable by everyone. When purchasing fresh fish I find the advice of the local fish merchant to be my best guide. Almost all fish are somewhat seasonal and your fishmonger is the one to tell you what's best at the moment.

When purchasing fish the primary thing, of course, is to make sure it's absolutely fresh. When you see it in the fish market or store it should be on ice, and it should have been there from the time it was caught. When you take it home it should be kept as cold as possible, without freezing, in your refrigerator. One way to judge freshness easily is that the fish simply does not smell objectionable ... fishy, yes, but not objectionably so. When you press down on the fish it should spring back; the eyes should be clear and bright; the scales should still be shiny and colourful.

Allow a whole pound to a person when buying a whole fish, and when buying fillets or steaks allow between $\frac{1}{3}$ and $\frac{1}{2}$ lb depending on your appetites. In these portions you will be getting vitamin A, all the vitamin D you can use, and sometimes vitamin C, thiamine, riboflavin, and nicotinic acids, plus all those minerals I mentioned earlier!

Frozen fish are generally sold in the form of steaks or fillets. I have my best luck letting them thaw very slowly in the refrigerator, but of course this involves preplanning that is not always possible. In any case, always have your fish or shellfish completely thawed before cooking.

As a general rule, fish requires much more delicate cooking than any other protein source. Since it has no tough fibres to break down, it requires less time and when over-cooked quickly becomes dried-out and tough. Testing with a fork for flaking, which means that the natural sectioning of the flesh of the fish separates easily, is the usual rule-of-thumb. Fish with a higher fat content – such as salmon,

75

mackerel, and albacore – lend themselves best to broiling and baking; others such as sole and sea bass lend themselves well to poaching.

However, almost all fillets and steaks lend themselves to being sautéed, and to me this is one of the easiest and most delicious ways to serve fish. Simply take rather thin fillets or steaks, dredge them very lightly in flour, and pan-fry them in margarine for a very few minutes. (I usually mix a little corn oil in with the margarine . . . it seems to brown better without burning.) Grilled fish should generally be basted with the same combination, after the same flour-dusting treatment.

Fish such as fillet of sole or salmon steak, cooked easily and quickly this way, served with a baked potato and another vegetable, constitutes what I might designate as our basic arthritic's dinner, and roughly what you should stay with until you get results.

I suggest that you always prepare every other part of the meal first, and leave yourself absolutely free to concentrate on the fast, light touch with your fish.

SHELLFISH

Some of the easiest and most elegant ingredients of this diet are the shellfish. Lobster, crab, and shrimp are so good by themselves that they can be boiled and served with a bowl of safflower oil mayonnaise, a green salad, and a loaf of French bread. There are, of course, innumerable ways to serve these delicacies, some of which follow, but to my mind nothing surpasses the aforementioned method.

CRACKED CRAB

This is the greatest feast; crab must be fresh to eat this way. It is cooked in boiling water and chilled, the claws are broken off the body and cracked, and the body is cut in pieces. Serve it on a bed of cracked ice to keep it very cold. A big bowl of safflower oil mayonnaise, and French bread, are called for, and you may complete the meal with a green salad.

FRESH CRAB

To my mind this is the best way to serve really fresh crab if you want a hot dish. Simply pile the crab in baking shells, pour melted margarine over it, and bake exactly 8 minutes in a hot oven (450 degrees or Reg. 8).

BAKED CRAB IN SHELLS

½ lb fresh crab meat
½ pt safflower oil mayonnaise
½ teaspoon tarragon
Pinch dry hot mustard
About 1 teaspoon dry white wine (cheating again, but just enough to flavour)
Breadcrumbs

Mix the crab meat, mayonnaise, tarragon, mustard, and wine; place in baking shells; top with the breadcrumbs; dribble with melted margarine; and slide under grill for about 5 minutes or until nicely browned. This makes a nice rich first course.

CRAB PILAF

2 pre-cooked crabs
¼ pt olive oil

1 *onion, sliced*
1 *pt water*
$\frac{3}{4}$ *pt clam juice or fish stock*
1$\frac{1}{2}$ *teaspoons salt*
$\frac{1}{2}$ *lb uncooked rice*
3 *tablespoons chopped fresh mint leaves*

Crack the crabs. Heat the oil in a heavy pan that has a tight lid, and sauté the onions till soft. Add the water, clam juice or stock, and salt, and when boiling add the rice and mint. Cover, reduce the heat, and simmer slowly about 45 minutes. About 10 minutes before the rice is done, stir in the crab and remove the lid. In Greece this dish is cooked with tomatoes, but I found it to be very good cooked to our restrictions.

COLD BOILED LOBSTER

1$\frac{1}{2}$ *to* 2 *lb lobster*
1 *tablespoon chopped chives*
$\frac{1}{4}$ *teaspoon each tarragon, parsley, and chervil*
Pinch dry mustard
5 *tablespoons safflower oil mayonnaise*
3 *tablespoons olive oil*

Boil the lobster, and either remove the meat from the shell and slice it or serve it in the shell. Mix all the other ingredients into a sauce, adding the oil last, gradually, to thin it.

STUFFING FOR GRILLED LOBSTER

3 *oz breadcrumbs*
$\frac{1}{4}$ *lb chopped clams*
$\frac{1}{4}$ *pt clam juice or fish stock*

Mix everything together and stuff into the cavity in the lobster shell. Or add to the breadcrumbs: the coral (roe), the long, green liver, and about 2 oz melted margarine.

CREAMED LOBSTER

¼ lb lobster meat
2 tablespoons flour
1½ oz margarine
¾ pt clam juice or fish stock
A few teaspoons of sherry!

Make a cream sauce from the *roux* of flour and margarine, gradually adding the liquid. Heat the lobster in the sauce and add the sherry. You are cheating, but everyone has to cheat a tiny bit once in a while, and this is *so* good.

LOBSTER AND CRAB PATTIES

¼ lb lobster meat
¼ lb crab meat
1 oz margarine
1 tablespoon flour
¼ pt water
¼ pt safflower oil mayonnaise
1 teaspoon salt
Pinch nutmeg
3 oz breadcrumbs
6 tablespoons peanut oil

Remove all pieces of shell from the freshly cooked crab and lobster. Cut into nice bite-sized pieces. Make a *roux* of the margarine and flour, add the water to make a smooth, thick sauce, and remove from the stove. Stir in the mayonnaise, salt, and nutmeg; add the seafood. Cool at room temperature, chill in the refrigerator about 10 minutes, and shape into rissoles. Roll in the bread crumbs, and fry in very hot peanut oil in a large frying pan. Drain on absorbent paper.

SHRIMPS

Shrimps happen to be one of the mainstays of my daily sustenance. They're easily available, and in their different forms and sizes can be prepared in a great variety of ways. Shrimps can be purchased all cooked and ready to eat, and they make a perfect luncheon salad, either with just lettuce and safflower oil mayonnaise, mixed with chopped celery and spring onions, or surrounded by cold vegetables with a garlic oil dressing. Tinned shrimps could be used the same way.

Prawns are of the same family, though I find people in different parts of the country differ widely in what they consider a prawn. I am speaking of the very large raw shrimps, around 3 inches long before shelling. They're expensive and utterly delicious. They must be cooked delicately and briefly, and I don't like to spoil their flavour with too much seasoning of any kind. To remove the vein insert a toothpick into the back, about midway, and pull it out. If it breaks, repeat in a different spot.

GRILLED SHRIMPS

2 *lb shrimps* (*the regulation-size shrimp, not the tiny ones or the prawns*)
1 *teaspoon salt*
3 *tablespoons chopped parsley*
2 *cloves garlic*
$\frac{1}{2}$ *pt olive oil*
1 *tablespoon basil*

Shell the shrimps and make a marinade of the other ingredients. Marinate the shrimps as long as possible, overnight perhaps, in a closely covered container in the refrigerator. To cook, place them in a shallow pan, pour the sauce over them, and grill under a brisk flame 5 to 8 minutes. Serve with the remaining marinade as sauce.

SHRIMP SPAGHETTI-TETRAZZINI

2 *oz margarine*
1 *bunch spring onions, thinly sliced and including a little of the tops*
$\frac{1}{4}$ *pt cold water*
4 *tablespoons cornflour*
1$\frac{1}{2}$ *pts chicken broth*
$\frac{1}{2}$ *pt clam juice or fish stock*
$\frac{1}{2}$ *teaspoon oregano*
2 *tablespoons corn oil*
2 *cloves garlic, crushed*
$\frac{1}{2}$ *lb mushrooms, sliced thin*
$\frac{1}{2}$ *lb spaghetti*
2 *lb cooked medium shrimps*
Salt

Melt half the margarine in a heavy pan. Add the spring onions and the water. Cook until the water has boiled away and the onions are soft. Add the cornflour (which has been mixed with a little cold water) and stir for 1 minute; then add the chicken broth, stock, and oregano. Stir constantly until it begins to boil; then set the pan aside. Heat the remaining margarine in the oil over high heat, and add the garlic and mushrooms. Toss and shake the pan until the mushrooms have browned – about 5 minutes.

Cook the spaghetti according to the directions on the packet; drain well. Mix all the ingredients together in a large,

81

shallow casserole and bake in a 375-degree or Reg. 4 oven about 15 minutes, or until the top is nicely browned.

INDONESIAN NASI GORENG

½ lb rice
1 large onion, chopped
1 clove garlic, crushed
½ lb small shrimps
Vegetable oil
Soya sauce

Boil the rice until done. Sauté the onions and garlic in the oil until golden; add the rice and shrimps. Heat through and add soya sauce to taste.

PRAWNS

I am very fond of prawns sautéed in a lot of margarine with their shells on. Devein them as described on page 80, rinse and dry them, and sauté them in hot bubbling margarine just until they're quite pink. This is a messy way to eat them, since you must remove the heads and shells with your fingers, but it's delicious.

Another way is to shell them beforehand, finely chop some onion and green pepper, and sauté that first. Then when you add the prawns include some chopped basil and a tiny piece of crumbled bay leaf.

SHISH KEBAB

Scallops
Prawns

Green peppers, cut in hunks
Quartered onions
Large whole mushrooms

Use about two of each item per person. Marinate everything in olive oil and crushed garlic, bay leaf, tarragon, and oregano. Thread on skewers and barbecue or grill.

SAUTÉED OYSTERS ON TOAST

$\frac{1}{2}$ *pt clam juice or fish stock*
1 *dozen oysters, fresh or canned*
French breadcrumbs, salted

Dust the oysters with flour and let stand 15 minutes. Dip in stock and again let stand 15 minutes. Roll in breadcrumbs. Sauté in generous amount of margarine until golden brown and crispy. Serve on toast made from wholewheat bread. Sprinkle with freshly chopped parsley.

SCALLOPED OYSTERS

2 *glass jars (about* 10 *oz each) fresh oysters*
2 *oz melted margarine*
6 *oz breadcrumbs*
Salt

Drain the oysters; dry them carefully on paper towels. Dip each oyster in the melted margarine; then roll it in the breadcrumbs till completely covered. Lay in a casserole, salting rather generously, and bake in a 350-degree or Reg. 3 oven for 30 minutes.

CLAM SPAGHETTI

Two 8-oz tins minced clams
1-lb packet thin spaghetti
2 oz margarine
3 tablespoons oil
1 clove garlic, crushed
1 onion, chopped
Salt

Sauté the onion and garlic in 1 oz margarine – do not brown. Add the juice from the clams; salt and simmer about 20 minutes. Add the clams just before serving; heat only long enough to make good and hot. Boil the spaghetti, meanwhile, in a large amount of well-salted water, making sure the strands are well separated. Cook *al dente*, in other words till firm to the bite, which should be 9 or 10 minutes. Drain off most of the water, but be sure to leave about ¼ pt. This is the secret of good spaghetti. Add the other 1 oz of margarine and serve with the sauce.

Very often in winter we simply make the sauce, add a tin of clam juice or stock, and serve it as a soup with croutons made of cubed French bread fried in margarine.

AUBERGINES STUFFED WITH CLAMS

1 large aubergine
½ minced onion
2 oz margarine
8-oz tin minced clams
2 tablespoons minced parsley
½ teaspoon minced basil
1 cup soft French breadcrumbs

Cut the top from the aubergine and scoop out the insides, being careful to leave enough shell to hold the filling. Chop the insides and cook in your French steamer until tender. In another pan sauté the onions in the margarine; add the cooked aubergine, clams, and herbs, and fill the aubergine shell. Sprinkle with some buttered crumbs and bake 30 minutes at 350 degrees or Reg. 4. I think this is nice for a Sunday luncheon dish.

CLAM STEW

4 *carrots*
½ *lb peas, fresh or frozen*
6 *small new potatoes*
6 *small white onions*
4 *stalks celery, scraped and sliced*
12-oz *tin clam juice*
1-*lb tin creamed corn*
2 *bay leaves*
Basil, rosemary, thyme
Four 8-oz *tins minced or chopped clams*
4 *oz margarine*

Peel and cut up the vegetables; season and cover with clam juice, adding water as necessary to barely cover all the vegetables and seasonings. Simmer until tender; add the clams and margarine. Place in a casserole and cover the top with rounds of toasted French bread.

CLAMS AND RICE, WEST COAST U.S.A. STYLE

2 *lb steamed clams*
1 *large bunch spring onions, thinly sliced*
1 *clove garlic, crushed*

1 *oz minced parsley*
1 *oz finely chopped seeded green pepper*
3 *tablespoons corn oil*
½ *lb rice*
¾ *pt water*

In a heavy pan sauté the spring onions, garlic, parsley, and pepper in the oil. When tender stir in the rice; then add the water and clams. Cover tightly and cook over medium heat till the rice is cooked – about 20 minutes. Taste for seasoning and serve in soup plates sprinkled with chopped parsley.

COQUILLES ST JACQUES

1 *lb scallops*
1 *pt water with small bay leaf, pinch thyme, few sprigs parsley*
1 *tablespoon chopped parsley*
Bunch spring onions, chopped
1½ *oz margarine*
Salt
½ *oz flour*
Breadcrumbs

Wash and drain the scallops. If large cut into pieces; if small leave whole. Simmer in the water till tender, about 5 or 6 minutes. Remove with a slotted spoon, set aside, and boil the water rapidly till reduced almost by half. If you're a garlic lover, crush in 2 cloves garlic. Add the spring onions and parsley; simmer in the liquid 10 minutes. Make a *roux* of the flour and margarine; gradually add the liquid; salt to taste. After you have a nice creamy sauce, stir in the scallops, place them in baking shells, top with breadcrumbs, dot with margarine, and slide under the grill until nicely browned.

SAUTÉED SCALLOPS

Scallops are perhaps the most delicate of seafoods. They need only the quickest cooking and the simplest of seasonings.

1 *lb scallops, either fresh or frozen and thawed*
1 *oz margarine*
3 *tablespoons water*
1 *tablespoon dry white wine*
2 *tablespoons minced parsley*
Salt

Wash the scallops; dry carefully with paper towels; flour very lightly. Melt the margarine and add the scallops a few at a time, browning carefully on all sides. Immediately add the rest of the ingredients and stir carefully with a wooden spoon for a few minutes until they are heated through.

SCALLOPS IN BAKED POTATOES

2 *to 3 lb sea scallops*
6 *baking potatoes*
4 *oz margarine*
2 *teaspoons minced onion*
Salt to taste (takes quite a lot)
Dash Worcestershire sauce
2 *tablespoons cornflour*
1 *lb cooked green peas*

Cover the scallops with boiling water, add salt, and cook very gently about 12 minutes. Drain and save the broth. Pierce the potatoes with a fork and rub with margarine; bake 1 hour in a 400-degree or Reg. 4 oven. Melt the margarine, add the onion and Worcestershire sauce, blend in the corn-flour (moistened with a little cold water), and gradually add enough of the reserved broth to make a thick sauce. Salt to taste, add the scallops and peas, and serve over the baked potatoes.

FRIED SCALLOPS

Dip the scallops in clam juice or stock, roll in yellow corn meal, and deep-fry in corn oil till golden brown. Serve with a safflower oil mayonnaise sauce to which you've added diced cucumbers and minced spring onions. Or you may arrange the scallops in a shallow pan and bake in a 425-degree or Reg. 6 oven about 10 minutes.

SCALLOPS PROVENÇAL

1½ lb scallops
Flour, salted
6 tablespoons corn oil
2 cloves garlic, crushed
1 oz chopped parsley

Dust the scallops with the flour; heat the oil and add the garlic and scallops. Cook quickly, tossing and shaking the pan; salt to taste and add the chopped parsley.

SCALLOPS AMANDINE

1 lb scallops
Flour
2 oz margarine
2 tablespoons chopped parsley
1 oz slivered toasted almonds

Cut the scallops into bite-size pieces if large; dust with flour and brown in half the margarine till crisp and golden. Arrange on a heated serving dish. Melt the remaining margarine, add the almonds and parsley, and pour this over the scallops.

WHAT TO DO WITH SALMON

As I happen to consider salmon the king of fish, I like to devote some loving care to its preparation. If you are lucky enough to get it fresh, it just has to be the most delicious thing there is!

When you have a whole salmon, proceed in this manner: Of course it must be cleaned – something I always leave to someone else. However, I have the head left on, but I remove the gills myself. For some reason they have a bitter flavour. Rinse and dry the fish well, rub it all over with margarine, and wrap it securely in aluminium foil. Put it in a baking dish and bake it 10 minutes a pound in a 350-degree or Reg. 4 oven. Allow cooling time before serving, because it takes about 10 minutes for it to cool enough to make the skin slide off. When it is completely free of skin, slide it on to a platter and carefully cut off the head. Use your imagination with cucumber and lemon slices, green and ripe olives, and sprigs of parsley. Salmon is marvellous either hot or cold, and when it's cold I also like to serve safflower oil mayonnaise mixed with chopped chives and parsley.

SALMON CHAUD-FROID

A really elegant way to present a salmon for a Sunday lunch or even as a first course at your very fanciest dinner is to glaze it with a chaud-froid. In the first place, have your salmon as smooth as possible. In this case you might refrigerate it before removing the skin because you're serving it cold anyway. Now soften 2 tablespoons unflavoured gelatine in a cup of your chicken stock and dissolve it over hot water. Blend this with 1 pt safflower oil mayonnaise and watch it like a hawk. In about 15 minutes it will begin to thicken, and when it's just setting – not stiff but not so thin that it will run off the fish – pour it over the fish so that it coats it evenly. Don't try to smooth out any places with a knife; just pour the coating on and leave it alone. Refrigerate the fish and then decorate it suitably: a ripe olive slice for an eye, cucumber slices for the scales, parsley for the tail, etc. Of course, any whole fish can be prepared this way, but it's best for larger fish, which are easier to bone when serving.

SALMON STEAKS WITH BUTTER SAUCE

2 *lb salmon steaks* (4 *steaks if small*, 2 *if large*)
1 *tablespoon olive oil*
1 *oz margarine*
Salt
4 *shallots, minced*
4 *tablespoons water*
3 *oz margarine, chilled and cut into small pieces*

Marinate the fish in the olive oil 30 minutes, turning once. Grill 7 minutes on each side, and arrange on a hot serving dish. Keep warm. Sauté the shallots very gently in $\frac{1}{2}$ oz margarine until soft; add the water and reduce gently until 2 tablespoons of liquid remain. Remove the pan from the heat and beat in 2 pieces of the chilled margarine with a wire whisk. Return the pan to the heat and beat in the rest of the margarine piece by piece. Serve immediately.

I had what I think was the most perfectly cooked piece of salmon I have yet to taste at the Cypress Point Club at Pebble Beach, California. It was a fillet – the part towards the tail (the best) – and it had been brushed with a little oil and grilled. They'd dusted a little paprika on it so that it browned with a lovely crisp crust; it hadn't been turned, but their secret, as they told me, was that they'd turned off the grill and left it there for a while after it browned.

SALMON EN BROCHETTE

Chunks of fresh salmon 1½ to 2 inches square
Small onion, parboiled
Chunks of green pepper, parboiled
Fresh mushrooms, lightly oiled

Thread the fish and vegetables alternately on long skewers and slide the skewers under the grill. Grill, turning frequently, until the fish is easily flaked with a fork. Serve on a bed of rice to which you've added plenty of margarine.

SALMON MOUSSE

1½ tablespoons unflavoured gelatine
¼ pt cold water
6 oz cooked, flaked salmon
3 teaspoons grated onion
2 tablespoons capers
1 tablespoon soya sauce
1 cup safflower oil mayonnaise
Merest dash tabasco
Salt to taste

Soften the gelatine in the water and heat gently until dissolved; set aside to cool. Combine the other ingredients, fold in the cooled gelatine, and put in a 2-pt fish mould. This is nice served with thinly sliced cucumber mixed with safflower oil mayonnaise and a little dill weed.

91

FILLET OF SOLE

This is probably the most available and adaptable fish for general use. It's not too expensive and almost all markets have it in either fresh or frozen form. The varieties of ways to serve it are practically infinite; furthermore, there are quite a few different kinds of sole. In the first place, the real sole is a European fish, but we call our flounder, lemon sole, grey sole, dab, and petrale all by the general name of sole. Petrale and grey sole are perhaps the best, since they hold together in cooking better than lemon sole or flounder, but all are good.

I have a heavy aluminium shallow baking dish that is perfect for the cooking of sole. It's not quite 2 inches deep, and is long and narrow to accommodate the shape of the fillet.

SOLE AMANDINE

1½ *oz slivered almonds*
2 *tablespoons sliced shallots*
6 *tablespoons margarine*
1½ *oz blanched almonds pulverized in the blender*
1½ *lb sole fillets*
¼ *pt clam juice or fish stock*
1 *tablespoon cornflour*

Sauté the shallots for just a few minutes in a little of the margarine, stir in the almonds with the rest of the margarine, and add salt to taste. Smooth this paste on one side of each fillet and lay the fillets in a margarined shallow fish casserole. Pour the clam juice or stock around them (and if you're quite well now, add a little white wine). Bake till the fish separates easily with a fork, about 20 minutes, in a 350-degree or Reg. 4 oven. Remove the fish from the liquid, boil the liquid down to about ½ pt, and blend in the cornflour. When this is thickened add the slivered almonds, pour over the fillets, and serve.

SOLE BONNE FEMME

¼ *lb fresh mushrooms, chopped*
1 *tablespoon minced shallot*
3 *tablespoons parsley*
1½ *lb sole fillets*
½ *pt court bouillon*

Mix the mushrooms, shallot, and parsley, and spread on the bottom of the margarined shallow casserole or pan. Salt the fillets, arrange them on the mushrooms, and pour the court bouillon over all. Cook about 20 minutes in a 350-degree or Reg. 4 oven, remove the fillets (keep them warm), and reduce the sauce to about ½ pt. Add 1 oz margarine and pour over the sole. Garnish with parsley sprigs and serve.

SOLE MEUNIÈRE

6 *sole fillets*
Flour
3 *oz margarine*
3 *tablespoons corn oil*
Chopped parsley

Dredge the fillets lightly in flour; season with salt. Melt the margarine with the oil in a heavy skillet and sauté the fillets rather quickly, turning once. When nicely brown remove the fish to a hot serving platter, add 1½ oz more margarine and the chopped parsley to the pan, and pour everything in the pan over the fish.

GRILLED FILLETS OF SOLE

4 *tablespoons olive oil*
3 *shallots, minced*
1 *clove garlic, crushed*
1 *teaspoon basil*
1 *teaspoon salt*
2 *tablespoons chopped parsley*
6 *sole fillets, rather large, firm ones*

Sauté the shallots and the garlic in the oil and add the seasonings. Simmer about 5 minutes. Brush the fillets with oil and place under the grill. Grill 5 minutes, turn, pour the sauce over them, and continue grilling another 4 or 5 minutes until the fish is done.

GRILLED SOLE WITH HERBS

6 *sole fillets*
1½ *teaspoons salt*
2 *oz margarine*
2 *tablespoons chopped chives*
2 *tablespoons chopped parsley*
1 *teaspoon tarragon*

Place the fillets on an oiled grill rack and spread with the mixture of the other ingredients. Grill about 4 minutes on each side.

SOLE IN BREADCRUMBS

6 *sole fillets*
2½ *oz French breadcrumbs*
1 *teaspoon salt*

94

1 *tablespoon chopped parsley*
1 *tablespoon fresh dill or tarragon* (1 *teaspoon if dried*)
½ *pt clam juice or fish stock*
Flour
3 *oz margarine*
3 *tablespoons safflower or corn oil*

Mix the crumbs, herbs, and salt. Dip the fillets in the stock, roll lightly in the flour, dip in the liquid again, and then roll in the crumbs. Sauté till browned (about 7 minutes) in the oil and margarine.

FILLETS OF SOLE NIÇOISE

2 *cloves garlic, crushed*
1 *onion, chopped fine*
1 *teaspoon salt*
1 *teaspoon rosemary*
About 20 *pitted large black olives*
18 *anchovies*
2 *tablespoons chopped parsley*
3½ *oz margarine*
6 *good-sized sole fillets*
½ *pt of clam juice or fish stock*

Combine the stock, 1 clove garlic, the onion, the salt, ½ teaspoon rosemary, and 2 oz margarine in a pan and bring to a boil. Reduce heat and simmer 15 minutes. Add 8 of the olives and reduce heat to very low while preparing the fish. Chop the anchovies and remaining olives and add the remaining garlic clove. Blend into this mixture the remaining margarine and rosemary and the parsley. Spread each fillet with some of the mixture; roll it up and secure it with toothpicks. Place the fish in a shallow dish just large enough to accommodate them, and pour over them the sauce.

95

Poach the fillets till done by the fork test, about 15 minutes. Remove to an ovenproof serving dish, sprinkle with chopped parsley, and run under the grill for just a minute.

COLD POACHED FILLET OF SOLE

Poach the desired number of fillets in sufficient court bouillon to cover generously. Cool, then refrigerate. These can be served with several types of safflower oil mayonnaise: one mixed with grated cucumber and dill, or one mixed with herbs such as tarragon and greens such as chopped spinach, watercress, and parsley.

SOLE FILLETS IN BAKED POTATO

4 or 5 oval-shaped potatoes
2 oz small shrimps
1½ oz margarine
Salt to taste
Handful chopped parsley
¾ pt cream sauce (made of 2 tablespoons flour, 1 oz margarine, and the poaching stock)
4 or 5 sole fillets
½ bay leaf
1 slice onion

Bake the potatoes in a 350-degree or Reg. 4 oven for 1 hour or till soft. Toss the shrimps in ½ oz margarine; season with the salt and parsley. Fold the sole over and poach in just enough water to cover, adding the bay leaf and onion. Now slice the top off each potato and scoop out some of the inside. Put shrimps in each, and add a fillet. Add the sauce and replace the top of the potato.

FILLET OF SOLE WITH SHRIMP SAUCE

4 *portion-sized sole fillets*
½ *lb small shrimps, or the tinned equivalent*
1 *carrot*
1 *onion*
1 *celery stalk*
1 *bay leaf*
1 *clove*
A little thyme
1 *tablespoon flour*
2 *tablespoons margarine*
About ¾ pt clam juice or fish stock
Paprika

Bring to a boil in a poaching pan about 2 inches water with the vegetables, herbs, and spices. Add salt, reduce heat, and poach the sole 5 or 6 minutes until it flakes with a fork. Make a *roux* of the flour and margarine, thin with the clam juice, add the shrimp, and mask the fish. Sprinkle with a little paprika and slide under the grill to brown nicely.

FILLET OF POMPANO

Boneless fillet of pompano (or other firm fillet)
2 *teaspoons finely grated fresh coconut*
1 *oz margarine*
3 *tablespoons slivered browned almonds*

Poach the fillet slowly in ½ inch water in a covered pan, for 5 minutes. Place under the grill covered with the fresh coconut; grill till the fish flakes with a fork. Serve with a sauce made of melted margarine into which has been beaten some of the poaching stock and the browned almonds and salt to taste.

FROG'S LEGS PROVENÇAL

8 *frog's legs*
2½ *oz margarine*
4 *cloves garlic, crushed*
2 *tablespoons fresh tarragon, chives, and parsley, finely chopped*

Wash the frog's legs; dry and dust lightly with salted flour. Melt the margarine and add the garlic. Cook 1 minute; then add the frog's legs and sauté till golden brown on both sides. Add the herbs, taste for seasoning, and cook just 1 minute more, or until a fork test shows they are done.

STUFFED TURBOT

4 *flat pieces of turbot*
½ *lb crab meat*
3 *tablespoons safflower oil mayonnaise*
1 *teaspoon mustard*
1 *tablespoon soya sauce*

Mix the crab with the condiments and arrange on the pieces of turbot. Roll up the pieces and fasten with toothpicks. Place them in a dish in which they will fit rather snugly and sprinkle lightly with paprika to brown. Bake in a 350-degree or Reg. 4 oven for 20 minutes.

TUNA LOAF

3 *slices French bread, crusts cut off (whole grain bread is good too)*
2 *family-size tins white chunky tuna (albacore)*

1 *small onion, grated*
Salt
½ *teaspoon thyme*

Soak the bread in a cup of water 30 minutes or so. Add the onion and seasonings, stir well, and add the tuna. Mix, place in a loaf tin, and press into loaf shape. It will stick together if you have enough bread in it and press it firmly enough. Bake in a 350-degree or Reg. 4 oven for 30 minutes or until brown and crisp on top.

AUBERGINE AND TUNA

Parboil the aubergine; split it and scoop out the pulp. Combine the pulp with a 7-oz tin of white tuna (albacore) and 2 tablespoons corn oil. Season with onion salt and chopped basil. Heat through in the oven.

TUNA CASSEROLE

1 *oz margarine*
1 *smallish onion, minced*
2 *tablespoons flour*
Two 7-oz tins white tuna (albacore)
¾ *pt clam juice or fish stock*
French Breadcrumbs

Melt the margarine and sauté the onion. Gradually work in the flour to make a smooth mixture; add the liquid gradually and stir till thick. Pour this over the tuna in a shallow casserole and top with French breadcrumbs. Bake in a 350-degree or Reg. 4 oven for 20 minutes.

TUNABURGERS

7-oz tin white chunky tuna (albacore)
¼ pt safflower oil mayonnaise
1 oz breadcrumbs
2 tablespoons finely chopped onions
2 tablespoons finely chopped green pepper
½ teaspoon oregano
Garlic salt

Mix well and press into rissoles. They should hold together, but if you have trouble, here's the place for the soya bean-flour egg yolk mentioned on page 29. Grill over charcoal, about 4 minutes on each side, putting aluminium foil under them if necessary to keep them from falling through the grill.

FISH STEW PROVENÇAL

5 medium potatoes, sliced
1 onion, sliced
2 cloves garlic, crushed
Salt
1 bay leaf
1 celery stalk, broken in half
2 large sprigs parsley
Pinch fennel seeds
5 tablespoons olive oil
2 lb fresh white-fleshed fish fillets, cut into large bite-sized
    pieces (you can have several varieties of fish, whatever you
    choose)

Arrange the fillets in a large, heavy saucepan. Cover them with the potatoes; add the onion and garlic. Add the seasonings and herbs, pour the olive oil over them, and cover everything with boiling water. Bring to a boil and simmer gently about 20 minutes or until the vegetables are tender. Remove the bay leaf, celery, and parsley before serving in large soup plates.

FILLET OF HADDOCK WITH CRAB SAUCE

About 1¼ lb haddock fillets
1 oz margarine
2 tablespoons onion juice
¼ teaspoon salt

Melt the butter; add the seasonings. Dip the fish in the mixture, flour very lightly, place in a shallow dish, and bake at 450 degrees or Reg. 8 for 20 minutes.

SAUCE

1 oz margarine
3 oz crab meat
2 tablespoons cornflour, mixed with a little cold water
¼ teaspoon salt
½ pt clam juice or fish stock
A suspicion of sherry

Sauté the crab meat in the margarine in a covered pan 5 minutes. Mix the dry ingredients and add them, stirring constantly. Add the liquid and, just at the last minute, the dash of sherry.

SCALLOPED FISH

6 pieces flounder or any other boned fish
4 large onions
1 lb fresh mushrooms
3½ oz French breadcrumbs
5 oz margarine

Chop the onions and mushrooms, sauté in the margarine, add the crumbs to make a thick paste, and season with salt. In a margarined casserole place a layer of the crumb mixture alternately with a layer of fish, topping with the crumb mixture. Bake in a 350-degree or Reg. 4 oven till the fish flakes with a fork, about 45 minutes to one hour.

STUFFED LAKE TROUT

Trout (weighing between 3 and 5 lb)
5 oz French breadcrumbs, fresh
1 small minced onion
1 tablespoon chopped parsley
Large pinch thyme
Pinch nutmeg
Salt
3 tablespoons clam juice or fish stock

Mix all the seasonings with the bread crumbs, add the liquid, and mix well. Stuff the trout lightly with this mixture, place in an oiled baking dish, and if you have dressing left place it over the fish. Bake in a 375-degree or Reg. 5 oven about 40 minutes. Garnish with parsley and fresh mint.

FRESHWATER FISH EN PAPILLOTE

Take a trout, or other small freshwater fish (cleaned, of course), and after wiping with a damp cloth salt it inside and out. Spread margarine over a large piece of waxed paper and wrap the fish securely, tying it if necessary. A little fresh chopped mint may be sprinkled on the fish before wrapping. Place in a shallow baking dish and bake in a 400-degree or Reg. 5 oven about 50 minutes. The time will vary according to the size of the fish. Fifty minutes is right for one weighing about 5 lb. Serve directly from the paper.

RAINBOW TROUT

These little wonders are best cooked in corn meal in the time-honoured way of the flycaster. If you've been lucky enough to catch them yourself, they'll taste wonderful no matter what you do to them, but they are available frozen in some markets, and properly defrosted first are quite acceptable. Rub them with salt, roll them in yellow corn meal, and sauté in a generous amount of margarine, allowing about 10 minutes to the first side and 5 to the second.

STEAMED FRESHWATER FISH

Use rock bass, lake trout, or whitefish, which have been wiped with a damp cloth and in which you have placed a clove of garlic and a bay leaf. Place the fish in a wire basket over a pan of water, cover the pan, and steam 15 minutes. Serve with this sauce; Cook together 2 tablespoons cornflour (moistened with water) and 1 oz margarine to make a *roux* and gradually add $\frac{3}{4}$ pt clam juice or fish stock and 4 tablespoons soya sauce.

STRIPED BASS

Striped bass are available from both the Atlantic and Pacific waters; they are different in colour but are essentially the same fish. Ask the fishmonger to bone them for you – it makes for much pleasanter eating.

HERB-STUFFED BASS

1 *whole striped bass, about 4 lb*
10 *oz French breadcrumbs, dry*
1 *large onion, minced*
2 *stalks celery, minced*
1 *teaspoon salt*
¼ *teaspoon thyme*
Pinch each tarragon and rosemary
3 *oz margarine*

Sauté the onion and celery in the margarine; add to bread-crumbs with the rest of the seasonings. Stuff the fish loosely and fasten with toothpicks or skewers; rub with margarine and place in an oiled baking dish. Bake 40 minutes in a 350-degree or Reg. 4 oven.

BASS WITH MINT AND GARLIC

1 *whole striped bass, about 4 lb*
¼ *pt olive oil*
1 *oz French breadcrumbs, dry*
1 *tablespoon minced parsley*
1 *teaspoon salt*
6 *sprigs fresh mint*
2 *cloves garlic, crushed*
1 *teaspoon chopped fresh basil, or pinch of dry*
¼ *pt clam juice or fish stock*

Mix the crumbs with the parsley, salt, and basil; add 2 tablespoons oil, the garlic, and the mint sprigs. Stuff the fish, securing with skewers, and place in a margarined baking dish. Pour the remaining oil over the fish and bake in a 350-degree or Reg. 4 oven for 40 minutes. Baste frequently with the pan drippings.

104

STUFFED STRIPED BASS, GREEK STYLE

I love the food in Greece – the fish is wonderful, and I used to wonder why I felt so marvellous there. It's understandable when you realize that the Greeks use the most basic ingredients, such as olive oil, onions, celery, nuts, and simple herbs.

1 *whole striped bass, 3 or 4 lb*
¼ *pt olive oil*
1 *tablespoon oregano*
2 *tablespoons chopped parsley*
Stuffing
Melted margarine
Salt

Have the fishmonger clean the bass, leaving on the tail. Salt the inside of the fish and fill with the stuffing described below (any remaining stuffing may be cooked in a covered casserole). Secure the fish with skewers and string, brush it with melted margarine, and place it in a baking dish. Combine the oil, parsley, and oregano and pour this over the fish. Bake 1 hour at 375 degrees or Reg. 5. Serve garnished with Greek olives.

STUFFING FOR BASS

1 *lb rice*
2¼ *pts clam juice*
3 *tablespoons chopped parsley*
3 *oz chopped onions*
3 *oz chopped celery*
3 *oz margarine*
2 *oz pine nuts*
Salt

Steam the rice in 2 pts clam juice 20 minutes. Sauté the onions, parsley, and celery in the margarine until golden;

add the rice and pine nuts, salt to taste, and add the remaining $\frac{1}{4}$ pt liquid.

HADDOCK OR COD WITH NUTS

3 lb haddock or cod steaks
$\frac{1}{4}$ pt olive oil
2 onions, chopped
2 tablespoons chopped parsley
$\frac{1}{4}$ pt water
1 tablespoon each walnuts, almonds, and hazel nuts, chopped in blender
2 tablespoons French breadcrumbs
$\frac{1}{2}$ pt court bouillon

Sauté the onions and parsley in the oil over a low heat. Add the fish steaks and water; simmer 15 minutes. In a separate pan brown the nuts, stirring constantly; add the breadcrumbs and stir until brown. Add the fish stock, and bring to a boil while continuing to stir. Pour the sauce over the fish, and serve with toasted French bread.

COD OR BASS WITH AUBERGINE

2 lb cod or bass fillets
1 aubergine
1 oz margarine

Slice the aubergine, salt each slice, and allow it to stand under a weight such as a heavy iron skillet for an hour. Drain away the resulting water. Sauté the fish and aubergine together in the margarine about 10 minutes. Serve with this Greek sauce:

106

SAUCE

4 *large cloves garlic, crushed*
1 *teaspoon salt*
½ *pt olive oil*
2 *oz toasted almonds*

COD OR SEA BASS WITH PINE NUTS

1½ *lb boned or filleted fish*
½ *lb chopped leeks*
2 *oz finely chopped onion*
1 *oz margarine*
2 *tablespoons olive oil*
1 *large clove garlic, crushed*
¼ *teaspoon thyme*
½ *teaspoon sage*
Salt
½ *pt clam juice or fish stock*
4 *tablespoons chopped parsley*

Sauté the leeks and onion in the oil and margarine; add the garlic and seasonings. Add the liquid and simmer uncovered about 30 minutes; add the parsley. Meanwhile, the fish has been quickly sautéed in oil until golden brown on both sides. Now arrange the fish in an oiled baking dish, pour the sauce over it, and sprinkle with pine nuts; bake 25 minutes in a 350-degree or Reg. 4 oven.

Polenta is good with this very Italian dish. Simply add 3½ oz corn meal slowly to 2 pts boiling water; boil, stirring, 5 minutes; add 2 oz margarine; and bake in a 350-degree or Reg. 4 oven until set, about 50 minutes.

ESCABECHE

2 *lb steaks or fillets of mild firm, white-fleshed fish (such as rockfish, halibut) about ½ inch thick*
Salt
Salad oil (not olive)
2 *large sweet onions, very thinly sliced*
9 *tablespoons olive oil*
2 *carrots peeled and grated*
½ *pt fish stock*
2 *cloves garlic, minced or mashed*
2 *bay leaves broken*
About 2 teaspoons salt
1 *teaspoon paprika*

Season the fish lightly with salt: let stand for 15 minutes. Quickly fry in generous amount of salad oil until the flesh loses translucency and flakes easily with a fork. Allow to cool; remove any skin and bones; break into large chunks. In a large frying pan sauté the onions in olive oil until limp. Stir in the carrots, stock, garlic, bay leaves, salt, and paprika. Allow to cool. Arrange the fish and the onion mixture in alternate layers in an earthenware jar or bowl or glass jar. Cover and chill at least 2 days. Makes 10 first course helpings or 6 supper helpings.

ITALIAN FISH CASSEROLE

2 *oz almonds*
2 *carrots*
Stalk celery
4 *oz mushrooms*
2 *medium onions*
1½ *lb codfish fillets*
Salt and margarine
½ *pt clam juice or fish stock*

Chop all the vegetables finely; mix together. Line a casserole with half the vegetables and lay the fish fillets on them. Add salt and cover with the remaining vegetables. Sprinkle with the chopped almonds, and moisten with about ½ pt clam juice or fish stock. Cover and bake 30 minutes in a 350-degree or Reg. 4 oven, removing the cover the last 10 minutes. Serve with margarined spaghetti or noodles.

CODFISH CAKES WITH SKORDALIA

1-*lb packet salt codfish*
1 *bay leaf*
1 *onion, quartered*
½ *lb mashed potatoes*
2 *spring onions, chopped fine*
2 *tablespoons finely chopped parsley*
2 *tablespoons olive oil*
1½ *oz margarine*

Prepare the codfish according to the directions on the packet, repeating the soakings and boilings at least four times. The last time add the bay leaf and onion to the pot and boil slowly 20 minutes. Drain, and remove the bay leaf and onion. If the cod is still salty boil again with cold water; drain. Place the fish in a colander; mash and squeeze it with your hands until all the water is removed and it is well mashed. Add the mashed potatoes, spring onions, and parsley; knead and shape the mixture into rissoles on a floured board. Dust them with flour and sauté in margarine and oil until golden brown. Serve with the following sauce.

SKORDALIA

6 *cloves garlic, crushed*
½ *lb mashed potatoes*
½ *teaspoon salt*
½ *pt olive oil*

Purée the garlic, potatoes, and salt in the blender till smooth; then slowly pour in the olive oil. If too thick, thin with a little water. Chill before serving.

COD IN CASSEROLE

2-*lb packet salt codfish*
4 *large potatoes, boiled and sliced*
3 *tablespoons minced parsley*
1 *teaspoon oregano*

Prepare the codfish as in the recipe for codfish cakes, but in this the codfish should be flaked instead of mashed. Place a layer of codfish flakes in an oiled casserole, add a layer of sliced potatoes, dot with margarine, top with a layer of codfish, and sprinkle with oregano and parsley. Cover with a white sauce made of 3 tablespoons flour, 2 oz margarine, and 1 pt clam juice or fish stock to which you have added 2 cloves crushed garlic. Bake in a 300-degree or Reg. 2 oven for 1 hour.

SHAD OR HERRING ROE

I really think shad roe is my all-time favourite in the delicacy department. Whenever I feel like going on a binge, I have shad roe – fresh when it's available, which is practically never, or tinned. Either way it's shamefully expensive. The following preparation is for fresh shad roe (the tinned I simply slide carefully into a little bubbling margarine and sauté gently till it's heated through, sometimes adding a little garlic).

2 *pairs shad roe*
1 *bay leaf*

110

1 *oz margarine*
1 *clove garlic, crushed*
1 *teaspoon minced parsley*

Place the shad roe in a pan and barely cover with water; add the bay leaf. Cook over a very low heat until the water comes to a boil; the gradual heating toughens the skin, hopefully keeping all the little precious eggs inside. Remove the shad roe from the water; drain and dry very carefully. Sauté in the margarine with the garlic and parsley until golden brown. When serving, pour the margarine remaining in the pan over the shad roe.

7

Chicken

As mentioned earlier, the white meat of chicken breasts may be added to the diet as an occasional change. I waited over a year before I tried it, but this is up to the individual's common sense. I've never noticed any ill effect from it, and its very versatility makes it a wonderful addition to our menus.

CHICKEN STEW

4 *chicken breasts*
¾ *pt water*
1 *oz margarine*
2 *tablespoons flour*
Pinch each thyme and rosemary
12 *small boiling onions, peeled*
½ *lb fresh mushrooms*

Sprinkle the chicken generously with salt and brown in the margarine, using a heavy skillet. Remove the chicken from the pan and blend the flour and herbs in the remaining margarine. When smooth, gradually stir in the water, and when the mixture comes to a boil, add the chicken and onions. Simmer 20 minutes; add the mushrooms; simmer 10 minutes or until everything is done.

BREAST OF CHICKEN WITH WILD RICE
(for 1 person)

1 *chicken breast*
1 *small onion*
1 *carrot*
1 *stalk tender celery*
Sliver of garlic
1 *large mushroom, chopped*
1 *tablespoon cornflour*
½ *oz margarine*
½ *pt chicken broth*
3½ *oz wild rice*

In a small pan make a cream sauce of the margarine, corn-flour, and broth. Bone and skin the chicken breast, season with salt, and place in a heavy margarined skillet. Add the onion, carrot, celery, garlic, mushroom, and cream sauce. Cover the pan and simmer slowly until the breast is done. In the meantime, soak and wash the wild rice; boil 20 minutes and keep warm over steam till the chicken is ready. At the last minute a whisper of sherry is a nice addition to the chicken before serving it over the mound of wild rice.

FRIED CHICKEN AND RICE

¼ *pt olive oil*
1 *frying chicken cut into serving pieces*
1 *small onion, chopped*
1 *clove garlic, minced*
⅛ *teaspoon saffron*
1¼ *pts chicken broth*
Salt
½ *lb uncooked rice*

¼ *lb mushrooms, sliced*
4 *artichoke hearts*
A few sliced pimentos (or green peppers)

Heat the oil; brown the chicken on both sides. Add the onion and garlic; fry for a few minutes, then add the saffron, dissolved in chicken broth; salt. Cover and cook 20 minutes. Add the rice; stir well; cover again and simmer 30 minutes longer or until all the liquid has been absorbed and the chicken is tender. Add the artichoke hearts and pimentos for the last 10 minutes of cooking.

BAKED CHICKEN WITH HERBS

6 *chicken breasts*
5 *tablespoons olive oil*
½ *teaspoon each thyme, basil, and marjoram*
1 *tablespoon fresh cut chives*
Flour and salt
1 *tablespoon minced parsley*

Wipe the breasts with a damp cloth. Place in a bowl and pour 3 tablespoons oil over them; sprinkle with the mixed herbs and chives. Cover and let stand in the refrigerator 3 or 4 hours. Lift the chicken from the marinade, dust lightly with flour, and brown 15 minutes in 2 tablespoons oil. Arrange the breasts in a large, shallow casserole in one layer; sprinkle lightly with salt. Mix the marinade remaining in the bowl with ½ pt water; add the parsley to it and pour this over the chicken. Cover and bake in a 375-degree or Reg. 5 oven for 30 minutes. Uncover periodically to see if the chicken is done; baste frequently with the marinade in the casserole.

CHICKEN MARENGO

6 *chicken breasts*
2 *oz flour*
1 *teaspoon tarragon*
1 *teaspoon salt*
4 *tablespoons olive oil*
1 *oz margarine*
¾ *pt water*
2 *cloves garlic, crushed*
¼ *lb mushrooms, thinly sliced*

Shake the chicken in a paper bag with the flour, salt, and tarragon. Save the remaining flour. Heat the oil and margarine in a heavy skillet and brown the chicken carefully. Transfer to a heavy casserole. Stir the remaining flour into the oil and margarine left in the skillet and when a smooth paste add the water and stir until thickened and smooth. Pour this sauce over the chicken, add the garlic and mushrooms, and bake 30 minutes in a 350-degree or Reg. 4 oven. Sprinkle with minced parsley before serving.

CHICKEN BREASTS WITH GARLIC

4 *large chicken breasts*
2 *heads fresh garlic (peeled by slapping with the flat side of a
    big knife)*
¼ *pt olive oil*
3 *stalks celery, sliced thin*
4 *sprigs parsley*
½ *teaspoon tarragon*
1 *teaspoon salt*
Pinch nutmeg

Pour the oil into a heavy casserole with a tight-fitting lid. Turn the breasts over in the oil; add the peeled garlic cloves, celery, and parsley; sprinkle the seasonings over this and mix everything together well. Put foil over the top of the casserole, put on the tight lid, and then put more heavy foil over the lid. You want to have the chicken sealed as completely as possible during the entire cooking time. Cook 1½ hours in a 375-degree or Reg. 5 oven, and serve with toasted French bread to eat with the soft garlic.

GREEK-STYLE CHICKEN

6 *chicken breasts*
1½ *pts water*
1 *teaspoon garlic salt*
1 *onion, sliced*
4 *stalks celery, sliced*
1 *bay leaf*
1 *tablespoon minced parsley*
Pinch poultry seasoning
1 *tablespoon flour*
2 *teaspoons cornflour*
4 *tablespoons cold water*

Remove the skin from the chicken breasts; place them in a covered pot with the water, seasonings, vegetables, and parsley. Simmer until tender, about a half-hour. Remove the chicken to a serving dish and keep it warm. Make a paste of the flour, cornflour, and cold water and stir it into the simmering broth. When thickened, pour it over the chicken.

8
Vegetables

Vegetables are your principal source of enzymes, vitamins, and minerals. If you're not particularly turned on by vegetables, I suggest you experiment until you find ones you like; vegetables are an absolutely essential element of this diet. Really, they *can* be interesting!

Many vegetables also contain protein – cabbage, carrots, celery, corn, green peppers, and all the bean family. The vital enzymes, which as I explained earlier do not function properly unless the vegetables are raw, are abundant in the unrefined vegetable oils and the leafy green vegetables, as well as in garlic and onions . . . and again, cabbage. Potatoes contain vitamin B-1 (thiamine), vitamin B-2 (riboflavin), niacin, vitamin C, and iron. You'd do well to include them often in your menu, baked or boiled.

Broccoli, asparagus, carrots, corn, lettuce, peas, spinach, string beans, parsley, and watercress are some of the vegetables rich in vitamin A. The vegetables having the B vitamins are dried peas and beans, lentils, beetroots, cabbage, corn, broccoli, and potatoes. (Peanuts, soya beans, sunflower seeds, brewer's yeast, and wheat germ are also rich in B.) Our best sources of vitamin C are potatoes, green peppers, brussels sprouts, and other green vegetables.

In addition to the vitamins supplied by vegetables there are all the minerals: calcium, chlorine, copper, iodine, iron, magnesium, phosphorus, potassium, silicon, sulphur, and zinc.

All the foregoing should convince you that vegetables are very important and not to be slighted. It happens that corn, cabbage, and baked potatoes are the vegetables my husband and I mutually enjoy the most, so they appear quite regularly on our table. However, I've gradually become quite addicted to all vegetables and find myself craving a raw carrot when in the old days it would have been a chocolate cream. I even find them quite beautiful to look at when properly prepared and presented; I like to see vegetables such as carrots and green beans cooked whole, particularly when young and attractive. And a platter of skilfully arranged raw vegetables can become a work of art.

COOKING VEGETABLES

I find a French vegetable steamer indispensable. The vegetables stay firm and crisp and retain their vitamins and minerals. I like carrots, green beans, cauliflower, or peas slightly undercooked and served with a little olive oil in which I've crushed a clove of garlic. Salt is pretty much the only seasoning vegetables need, but occasionally I add a little marjoram and thyme to green beans, a little dill to cucumber, or a little basil to most anything.

BAKED VEGETABLES

When you want to have a vegetable that will be ready at the last minute with no further attention needed, bake it.

Scrape baby carrots and place them in a heavy skillet with 2 oz of margarine and 2 crushed garlic cloves; cover tightly. Bake in a 350-degree or Reg. 5 oven for 1 hour.

You can do the same thing with beetroot.

Soak a cauliflower for 1 hour in salt water. Separate into flowerettes and place in a margarined casserole. Sprinkle with a little water and dot with an ounce margarine (or more, depending on the size of the cauliflower). Cover and bake in a *very* slow oven for $3\frac{1}{2}$ hours.

118

ARTICHOKES

Cut the stem off at the base of 4 artichokes; pull off any tough outer leaves; trim about an inch off the top; and clip each leaf to remove its sharp thorny tip. Stand the artichokes in a large saucepan and add about 1½ inches water. Add 1 tablespoon olive oil, 2 cloves, 1 bay leaf, and a liberal amount of garlic salt. Cover tightly and steam till one of the large leaves pulls off easily. Drain upside down and serve with safflower oil mayonnaise mixed with a little soya sauce.

ASPARAGUS WITH BASIL

2½ *oz soft French breadcrumbs*
3 *lb asparagus*
1 *small onion, minced*
1 *oz margarine*
2 *teaspoons chopped basil*
1 *teaspoon salt*

Cook the asparagus, uncovered, 5 minutes in a skillet with about ½ inch water; cover and continue cooking until the tough part of the stalk is tender. In a separate pan heat the margarine and brown the crumbs, onion, and basil. I always have an old Turkish towel handy for drying asparagus; simply lay it on the towel and fold the towel over to keep it warm till you want it. Anything served over it, such as this crumb mixture, is absorbed into the stalk and twice as tasty.

CURRIED GREEN BEANS

1 10-*oz packet frozen whole green beans*
3 *tablespoons safflower oil mayonnaise*
2 *tablespoons minced onion*
¼ *teaspoon salt*
Small pinch curry powder

Cook the beans as directed on the packet. Mix the remaining ingredients and stir into the well-drained beans; heat thoroughly, but not enough to let the mayonnaise separate. Again I must say that you don't add spices such as this pinch of curry powder until you've been feeling really well for quite a long time. Your body will be able to handle these after it's in a proper balance, but only in small quantities.

LIMA BEANS WITH SAGE

1 10-*oz packet frozen baby lima beans*
1 *oz margarine*
1 *teaspoon sage*
Garlic salt

Cook the beans according to the directions on the package, adding the sage to the water. When done, drain, not disturbing whatever sage wants to adhere to the beans; add the margarine and salt.

BRUSSELS SPROUTS WITH CHESTNUTS

Make a cross on 8 chestnuts. Boil them 45 minutes in salted water; cool and peel. Boil 1 lb brussels sprouts; mix with the chestnuts; add margarine, salt, and a dash of nutmeg.

BRAISED CELERY WITH MUSHROOM SAUCE

Cut fresh young celery in uniform-sized stalks. Place in a pan, cover with water, and add ¼ pt soya sauce. Braise slowly, covered, until tender. Meanwhile mince some very fresh mushrooms and sauté in a saucepan about 10 minutes, stirring. Add salt, a pinch of nutmeg, and a generous piece of margarine; cook over low heat, stirring often. Drain the celery and cover it with the mushrooms.

CABBAGE

Cut a tender new head of cabbage into eighths or quarters, depending on the size. Cook in a French steamer till it pierces with a fork – not very long. Pour over it melted margarine, in which you have crushed a few dill seeds.

SAUTÉED CABBAGE

Remove the core of a tender young cabbage. Cut in small squares and sauté over a high heat in lots of margarine for just about a minute. It will be just tender-crisp. Add salt, a little dill weed and a tablespoon or so of safflower oil mayonnaise.

TENNESSEE CABBAGE

Place 1½ oz margarine in an iron skillet and brown slightly. Add 1 small head shredded cabbage and stir well. Cover tightly and simmer 5 minutes. Stir again, cover, and simmer 5 minutes longer. Add ½ teaspoon salt and ¼ pt water in which you have dissolved 1 tablespoon cornflour; stir well.

121

Cover and simmer 3 or 4 minutes. Time is very important, since the cabbage may be spoiled by overcooking. Serve very hot.

CORN COOKERY

My husband and I absolutely adore corn, and it's a wonderful food. (Look at the peoples of the world who've lived well on maize . . . think of the white teeth of the Mexicans.) Here in California we're fortunate enough to be able to get it almost all year round, but the frozen corn, both on the cob and cut off, is very good. (Of course you will carefully read your labels so as to buy frozen vegetables to which NOTHING has been added.)

I've never been able to improve on the old-fashioned way of starting the corn on the cob in cold water, bringing it to a boil, and taking it off after 3 minutes. Another great favourite of mine, actually from my childhood, is corn cut off and lightly sautéed with slivered green pepper.

SAUTÉED CUCUMBERS

Peel the cucumbers, cut in strips, and remove the seeds. Sauté in margarine and a little salt 10 minutes. Blend in 1 teaspoon flour and add finely chopped parsley.

AUBERGINE CASSEROLE

1 *large aubergine*
4 *boiling onions*
2 *oz flour*
1 *oz margarine*
Breadcrumbs

122

Peel the aubergine and boil it in salted water; drain it thoroughly and mash it lightly. Sauté the onions in 1 heaped tablespoon margarine until soft. Make a *roux* of flour and margarine, mix all the ingredients together and salt generously to taste. Cover with crumbs, dot with margarine, and bake 20 minutes in a 350-degree or Reg. 4 oven.

FRIED AUBERGINE

Slice the aubergine, soak in cold water for 1 hour, drain with a weight on top, and dry carefully. Dust with flour which has been seasoned with a little basil and garlic salt, and fry in a mixture of $\frac{1}{4}$ pt olive oil and $\frac{1}{4}$ lb margarine until golden brown.

BRAISED ENDIVES

8 *endives*
2 *tablespoons melted margarine*
Salt

Arrange the endives in an oiled casserole. Pour on the margarine and salt, and add about 4 tablespoons water. Cover tightly and bake in a 350-degree or Reg. 4 oven for 45 minutes, or until the endives are tender.

PARSLEY TEMPURA

Mix 2 oz flour, 2 oz cornflour, $\frac{1}{4}$ teaspoon baking powder, $\frac{1}{2}$ teaspoon salt and $\frac{1}{4}$ pt of water; beat smooth. Dip large fresh parsley sprigs in this mixture and fry quickly in deep hot corn oil.

GREEN PEPPERS

3 *tablespoons olive oil*
2 *onions, sliced thin*
2 *green peppers, seeded and cut in strips*
1 *clove garlic, crushed*
1 *tablespoon chopped fresh dill, or ½ teaspoon dried dill weed*
Salt

Heat the oil in a frying pan that has a tight cover. Place the onions and green peppers in the pan, onions on one side and peppers on the other. Cover and steam over low heat 10 minutes. Add the rest of the ingredients, cover, and cook another 5 minutes.

GREEN PEPPERS STUFFED WITH AUBERGINE

2 *large green peppers*
1 *large aubergine*
6 *tablespoons olive oil*
1 *clove garlic, crushed*
1 *oz breadcrumbs*

Cut the green peppers in half lengthwise and remove the seeds. Drop into boiling water for a minute or so, drain, and arrange in a baking dish. Cut the aubergine in small cubes and combine with the garlic and oil. Sauté until lightly browned, about 10 minutes, and fill the pepper shells with the mixture. Sprinkle with the breadcrumbs, moisten with a little additional olive oil, and bake in a 375-degree or Reg. 5 oven for 30 minutes.

LEEK SOUFFLÉ

3 *large leeks, white part only*
4 *egg whites*
Pinch nutmeg
Salt
1 *oz margarine*

Cook the sliced leeks in a small amount of water until they are very tender. Drain off the water, add the margarine and seasonings, and mash thoroughly with a potato masher. Fold in the stiffly beaten egg whites, turn into a margarined soufflé dish, and bake 30 minutes in a 350-degree or Reg. 4 oven.

TINY BOILING ONIONS

Peel 12 or 14 boiling onions and cover them with fish stock. Add 2 tablespoons olive oil, a little thyme, and a bay leaf; simmer very slowly till tender. Remove the onions, strain and reduce the liquid, and salt to taste. Pour back on the onions and reheat. This is a nice accompaniment to fish.

STUFFED ONION SHELLS

1½ *oz margarine*
3 *tablespoons flour*
1 *pt chicken stock*
3 *very large onions*
12 *tiny boiling onions*
½ *oz margarine*
½ *oz bread crumbs*

125

Make a *roux* of the margarine and flour; gradually stir in the stock to make a thick, creamy sauce. Keep it warm. Boil the large onions in enough salted water to cover for about 25 minutes, or till tender. Drain and cut in half crosswise; remove the centres. Cook the peeled small onions till tender; drain and add to the sauce.

Melt the margarine in a small pan and add the breadcrumbs. Now put the big onion halves in a shallow baking dish, and fill the centres with the small onions in the sauce. Sprinkle with the crumbs and slide under the grill till nicely browned.

SPINACH NESSELRODE

1 *lb fresh spinach*
2 *lb fresh broccoli*
Safflower oil mayonnaise

Chop the vegetables as finely as possible. Bring 1 pt water to a boil with 1 teaspoon salt. Add the broccoli and boil 6 minutes; add the spinach and boil 4 minutes. Drain very thoroughly and immediately stir in enough mayonnaise to coat the mixture and hold it together.

RATATOUILLE

¾ *lb marrow*
3 *large cloves garlic, crushed*
6 *tablespoons olive oil*
1 *teaspoon cumin seeds, crushed*
½ *aubergine*
1 *teaspoon oregano*
3 *onions, sliced thin*
2 *green peppers, seeded and cut into strips*

½ *teaspoon marjoram*
½ *teaspoon dill weed*
Salt

Peel the aubergine, cut it into small cubes, salt it, and let it stand for a half hour or so. Cube the marrow and put it in the bottom of an oiled casserole. To this layer add salt, 1 clove garlic, 2 tablespoons of the oil, and the cumin seeds. Rinse and dry the aubergine, put it in the casserole, and to this layer add salt, another clove of garlic, and the oregano. Now add the onions and green peppers, the rest of the garlic and oil, the marjoram and the dill weed. Cover and bake in a 350-degree or Reg. 4 oven for 1 hour.

COURGETTES

8 *courgettes* (*zucchini*)
Salt
Onion salt
Basil

Slice the courgettes on the diagonal, not too thinly. Melt 1 oz margarine and add a garlic clove. When the margarine is hot, remove the garlic; add the courgettes and basil. Cover the pan and shake over high heat until you can hear liquid boiling in the pan. Turn the heat down, add the salt and onion salt, and continue cooking until the courgettes are crisp and firm.

SOUFFLÉ POTATOES

Peel potatoes and cut into thin slices. Wipe carefully with paper towels. Use two pans: a deep one with corn oil heated until it throws off a blue smoke and a heavy skillet with just

127

a little margarine melted in it. Put a few potatoes at a time in the skillet and let them just colour on both sides. Now remove them with a slotted spoon or spatula and drop them into the hot oil, just one or two at a time; they will puff like balloons. Sprinkle with salt and serve at once.

POTATOES ANNA

6 *large potatoes, peeled*
¼ *lb soft margarine*
½ *teaspoon salt*

Slice the potatoes very thin; soak in cold water; drain and dry. Sprinkle with salt, and line the bottom of a margarined casserole with them. Spread margarine over them, add another layer of potatoes, and keep alternating, ending with a top layer of margarine. Bake in a 450-degree or Reg. 8 oven about 45 minutes. To serve, invert the casserole on a platter and you should have a brown, moulded form.

CANDIED SWEET POTATOES

4 *large sweet potatoes, unpeeled*
3 *oz brown sugar*
1 *oz margarine*
Salt

Boil the potatoes until almost tender; then peel and slice. Place in a shallow baking dish; salt; cover with brown sugar; dot with margarine. Bake in a 350-degree or Reg. 4 oven about 20 minutes.

128

COOKING RICE

The Chinese method of cooking rice works very well for me. Simply bring to a boil twice as much water as the amount of rice you use; add salt and the rice; cover and simmer till all the water is absorbed and the rice is tender. I use brown rice because the nutrients haven't been polished away, and find this requires a little more water, since it requires more cooking time.

When serving rice with fish I find that clam juice or fish stock instead of water is very good, and sometimes I use chicken stock when serving it with chicken. When cooking wild rice I follow the directions on the packet, using stock as above, and sometimes adding a few herbs such as thyme or basil. A good handful of chopped parsley with a large dollop of margarine just before serving helps plain rice.

RISOTTO

½ lb rice
1 twist vermicelli, broken in small pieces
1 small onion, chopped
1½ pts water or broth

Brown the onion and vermicelli in margarine; add the rice and the water or broth. Cook over low heat or bake in a 350-degree or Reg. 4 oven until all the water is absorbed.

BIRYANI (Indian-style fried rice)

1 lb long-grain rice, thoroughly washed
¼ pt peanut oil
3 onions, peeled and minced
2 cloves garlic, crushed

1 *small piece ginger, minced*
¼ *teaspoon turmeric*
Salt

Boil the rice 10 minutes in 2 pts water, drain, and spread on a flat surface for quick cooling. Heat the peanut oil very hot; add the onions and ½ pt water. Cook over moderate heat until the onions are tender and all the water has boiled away. Stir in the rice, garlic, ginger, and turmeric; salt to taste. Add about 1 oz margarine and stir with a wooden spoon until the rice is done and looks fried.

9
Breads

Try making your own bread. Admittedly, there are now lots of good breads available that are free of additives and pre-servatives and are made from all natural ingredients. Again, read that label carefully to be sure you get no milk or eggs; you should be eating only the basic breads made from yeast, water, and unrefined flour, preferably whole-grain.

However, the smell of your own bread is worth the whole thing. Suddenly your house is more of a home, and everyone who enters knows it. The yeasty aroma that permeates your kitchen hangs on for days and sharpens appetites im-measurably.

Good bread should simply mean something out of the fields with nothing added but a little water and some fire and some skill. I've experimented with combinations of flours and grains such as rye and whole wheat, and come up with some nice Old World bread. Incidentally, my standard morning fare is tea with whole-wheat toast that is positively dripping in margarine and honey. One of the joys of this diet is that you get thin in spite of things like the afore-mentioned.

Fermented bread – made by mixing flour, water, salt, and yeast – is the easiest to make and the only kind, frankly, I've ever tried. For additional food value you may add malt extract or honey. The object in the kneading of the dough is to incorporate air into it, and it must be kneaded until it's elastic to the touch. When it's covered with a cloth and set aside to rise, it's important to have a warm, draught-free place. It so happens that the centre of my stove has a grill on it, and apparently the pilot light keeps it just about right. After the bread has risen, which takes from 2 to 4 hours, work it down again and turn it over in the bowl. And when it's risen again and you've worked out the air again and formed it into the loaves, leave them on the board a few minutes to let them rise a little. Be sure your oven is hot enough. As a general rule bread should be baked at high heat to start with, and after it has been thoroughly heated through, the heat is reduced. I always place a pan of water on a rack below the bread; the steam will keep it from burning.

WHOLE-WHEAT BREAD

1½ *pts warm water*
1 *cake compressed yeast*
2 *tablespoons Karo syrup*
1¾ *lb whole-wheat flour*
1 *tablespoon salt*

Dissolve the yeast in a little warm water, and mix all the ingredients. Turn out on a lightly floured board and knead at least 10 or 15 minutes. This is hard work, but keep thinking how good the bread's going to be. Then put it into a bowl, cover it with a dish cloth, and set it in a nice warm place to rise. After 2 hours tap it, quite sharply, and if it begins to sink it's ready.

Knead it again, and when it's well worked down return it to the bowl, cover it, and let it rise until it's half again its size. Shape it into loaves, put it into baking tins, and let it rise until it's half again its size. Bake it for 1¼ hours, starting at 450 degrees or Reg. 8, after 20 minutes reducing to 350 or Reg. 4, and then again reducing to 300 or Reg. 2. I like to brush the bread with melted margarine when I take it from the oven. Cool it on a rack.

FRENCH BREAD

2 *packets active dry yeast*
1 *pt warm water*
1¼ *lb sifted flour*
2 *teaspoons salt*
½ *teaspoon powdered ginger*
Corn meal

Add the yeast to the warm water in a large bowl. Stir till well dissolved. Add ½ lb flour, the salt, and the ginger; beat well with a large wooden spoon. Gradually beat in the rest of the flour, until the dough is very stiff. Knead on a floured board 8 to 10 minutes; cover your hands with margarine and pat the dough into a round ball. Place it in a bowl, cover it with a towel, and let it rise in a warm place till it doubles in size. Punch it down to break the rise, and shape into 1 large, long loaf or 2 smaller ones. (I make 2 long, thin, small loaves.) Dust a greased baking tray with corn meal, place the loaves on the sheet, and brush the tops with ice water. Cut the tops in slashes diagonally with scissors, and let the bread rise till doubled again. Place a pan of boiling water in the bottom of the oven. Bake the bread 7 minutes in a pre-heated 450-degree or Reg. 8 oven; then reduce the heat to 350 or Reg. 4 and bake for 35 minutes longer. Cool on a rack, after brushing the tops with margarine.

ROGGEBROOD (Dutch Bread)

7 *oz wheat bran*
6 *oz rye flour*
¼ *pt black molasses*
1 *teaspoon salt*
¾ *pt boiling water*

Stir everything together, and pack tightly into a 1-lb coffee can. Steam for 1¼ hours with the lid on the can in a pan of boiling water (there should be a lid on the pan also). Let the bread cool slightly and invert on a rack. Serve spread with margarine, but be sure to wait till it cools before attempting to slice it.

SOYA BEAN BREAD

2 lb whole-wheat flour
½ lb soya bean flour
1 cake compressed yeast
1 pt lukewarm water
6 tablespoons Karo syrup
Salt

Dissolve the yeast in a little warm water and mix all the ingredients into a good thick dough. Let it stand until double its size, in a nice warm place, and then knead it, lapping it over constantly towards the centre. Let it rise to half again its size, and knead it once more. Mould it into loaves, put it in baking tins, and let it rise again until double its size. Bake in a 450-degree or Reg. 8 oven, watching the browning and turning the heat down as necessary. Cool on a rack.

10

Desserts

Desserts are somewhat of a problem, since almost all contain eggs or cream or chocolate or something else that's *verboten*. However, after a short time on this regime I think you'll find, as I did, that your sweet tooth has dropped out. My husband and I never have desserts at all when we're alone, and these that I do make are mainly for entertaining. Somehow people expect something at the end of dinner or lunch, and one of the following recipes will fill the bill nicely.

My husband has his fruit and cheese anyway, but for the most part I think people now would rather have a pleasant surprise when they step on the scale in the morning.

ANGEL-FOOD CAKE

½ *pt egg whites*
¼ *teaspoon salt*
4 *tablespoons water*
1 *teaspoon cream of tartar*
½ *lb sugar*
¼ *lb cake flour*
1 *teaspoon almond extract*

Boil the sugar and water together until it forms a thread from the spoon. Beat the egg whites until stiff, gradually beat in the sugar mixture, then add the flavouring, and beat until cooled. Mix and sift the flour and other dry ingredients several times; then gradually fold in the beaten egg-white

135

mixture. Bake in an ungreased angel-food tin at 275 degrees or Reg. 1 for 30 minutes, then at 375 or Reg. 4 until the cake springs back when pressed with a finger.

MERINGUES WITH CHESTNUT PURÉE

4 *egg whites*
3 *oz fine granulated sugar*
Tin chestnut purée

Beat the egg whites till foamy; add the sugar gradually and beat until very thick. Drop in 6 rounds from a soup spoon on to oiled aluminium foil about 1 inch apart. Bake at 200 degrees or Reg. ¼ for 1¼ hours. Serve with tinned sweetened chestnut purée.

ALMOND OATMEAL CAKES

3 *oz margarine*
6½ *oz brown sugar*
4 *tablespoons water*
1 *generous teaspoon almond flavouring*
6 *oz flour*
½ *teaspoon baking soda*
1 *teaspoon salt*
6 *oz Quick Quaker Oats*
2 *oz finely chopped blanched almonds*

Mix the margarine, sugar, water, and flavouring and beat till smooth. Sift the dry ingredients together and add to the creamy mixture. Add the Quick Quaker Oats and the almonds. Drop by the teaspoonful on to greased baking sheet and slightly press down. Bake 14 minutes at 350 degrees or Reg. 4.

These cakes are even better when made with a product called Granola instead of the oats.

ALMOND MACAROONS

$\frac{1}{2}$-lb tin almond paste
6$\frac{1}{2}$ oz sugar
2 egg whites

Mix until very smooth. Squeeze through a pastry bag on to foil to form 1$\frac{1}{2}''$ small rounds. Bake at 325 degrees or Reg. 4 for 30 minutes.

SWEET ALMOND DESSERT

4 oz sugar
$\frac{1}{2}$ pt light corn syrup
4 oz melted margarine
4 egg whites, beaten
1 teaspoon vanilla
6 oz diced sweet almonds
Coconut cream (tinned)

Beat the sugar, corn syrup, margarine, and vanilla together; add the beaten egg whites and nuts and turn into a margarined 8-inch baking tin. Bake in a 375-degree or Reg. 5 oven for 35–40 minutes. Cool on a rack, spoon into dessert dishes and serve topped with cocoanut cream.

ANGEL CREAM

3 oz grated almonds
5 eggs whites
4 oz sugar
1 teaspoon vanilla

Beat the egg whites till stiff, add 3 oz sugar, and then gently fold in the remaining 1 oz. Add the vanilla and gently fold in the almonds (can be grated in the blender). This should be cold, but since it must be done at the last minute, I keep the ingredients in the refrigerator until ready to make it. It only takes a few minutes to do, and is delicious served in sherbet glasses.

SPICE CAKE WITH CARAMEL FROSTING

½ pt water
2 oz margarine
6½ oz brown sugar
½ teaspoon cinnamon
½ teaspoon allspice
Good pinch nutmeg
½ lb cake flour
1 teaspoon baking powder
2 oz chopped almonds and pecans

Boil the water, margarine, sugar, and spices 3 minutes; allow to cool. Sift the flour and baking powder twice and remeasure. Stir gradually into the boiled mixture, and when smooth add the chopped nuts. Bake in a greased ring mould for 1 hour in a preheated 325-degree or Reg. 3 oven. Make the following icing:

13 oz brown sugar
5 tablespoons water
1½ oz margarine
1 teaspoon vanilla

Stir till dissolved, cover and cook 3 minutes, uncover and cook without stirring till it forms a ball in cold water. Add the margarine and let cool slightly. Add the vanilla and beat till thick and creamy.

SESAME-SEED COOKIES

2 oz coconut
4 oz sesame seeds
12 tablespoons corn oil
6½ oz brown sugar
½ lb flour
½ teaspoon baking soda
1 teaspoon baking powder
½ teaspoon salt
Vanilla or almond extract, whichever you prefer

Spread the coconut and sesame seeds on a baking sheet and toast them lightly. Cream the oil and sugar and gradually sift in the dry ingredients. Add the vanilla or almond extract, and mix in the coconut and seeds. Bake on an oiled baking tray for about 12 minutes at 350 degrees or Reg. 4.

COCONUT SHERBET

6½ oz sugar
1 packet unflavoured gelatine
½ pt water
Two ½-lb tins coconut juice
2 teaspoons vanilla
¼ lb shredded coconut
2 egg whites

Mix ¾ of the sugar with the gelatine in a saucepan, add the water, and stir over low heat till the sugar dissolves. Mix in the coconut juice, vanilla, and coconut and pour into a shallow dish to freeze till solid. Then break up in a bowl and beat till light and fluffy. Whip the egg whites till they form a peak, add the remaining sugar, fold them into the sherbet mixture, and freeze in a covered container. Serve scooped into balls, either passed in a silver bowl or in sherbet glasses.

11
Chinese Cooking

Chinese cooking is a delightful change from our daily fare, lends itself beautifully to our diet, of course, and is very quick and easy once you get the hang of it. But first you must get a wok, a conical heavy steel pan. Follow the directions concerning its seasoning, and with a wooden spoon and spatula you're ready to go.

CHICKEN AND MUSHROOM SOUP

1 *chicken breast*
1 *oz dried mushrooms*
2 *pts chicken broth*
½ *teaspoon salt*
1 *teaspoon cornflour*
1 *oz bamboo shoots*

Slice thinly the chicken and mushrooms. Moisten the cornflour with a little chicken broth, add the salt, and marinate the chicken. Put the 2 pts broth in the wok, add the mushrooms and bamboo shoots, and bring to a boil; then remove from the heat and add the chicken very carefully – you don't want to lose the cornflour. Return to the heat, and when the broth has once again reached the boiling point, test to see if the chicken is done. It should be just about right to serve in perhaps 30 seconds' boiling time.

PRAWNS

The wok lends itself admirably to cooking prawns. They may be either shelled beforehand or cooked in their shells and served that way.

PEELED PRAWNS

½ *lb prawns, deveined with a small toothpick poked under the middle of the back (the whole vein should lift out) and shelled*
1 *tablespoon clam juice or fish stock*
1½ *tablespoons soya sauce*
2 *teaspoons brown sugar*
Fingernail-sized piece ginger root
1 *spring onion, cut in 1-inch pieces*
1 *teaspoon cornflour*
1 *tablespoon safflower or corn oil*

Put the oil in the wok and when hot roll it around to coat the sides; add the prawns. Brown quickly on both sides, add the rest of the ingredients except the cornflour, cover with water, and cook for 10 minutes with a lid on. The heat should be just enough to keep the liquid boiling gently. Remove the lid and continue to cook, stirring, until the liquid has been reduced by half. Thicken with the cornflour, which has been moistened with a little water.

PRAWNS IN THE SHELL

½ *lb prawns, deveined but not shelled*
1 *spring onion, chopped*
Fingernail-sized piece ginger root

½ *clove garlic*
1 *teaspoon safflower or corn oil*
A little wine
1 *teaspoon brown sugar*

Put the oil in the wok and when hot add the prawns and fry for 2 or 3 minutes. Remove the prawns from the wok and put in the spring onion, ginger root, and garlic. Put back the prawns, stirring and shaking the wok constantly to allow the seasonings to reach all the shells. Sprinkle with a little wine several times to keep from burning, and add the sugar just as the prawns are done. There should be no liquid left in the wok.

SAUTÉED PRAWNS WITH BLACK-BEAN SAUCE

1 *lb prawns, washed, shelled, deveined, and cut into bite-size pieces*
2 *spring onions, diced*
1 *slice ginger, minced*
2 *tablespoons black beans*
2 *tablespoons soya sauce*
4 *tablespoons peanut oil (or any vegetable oil)*
1 *teaspoon cornflour, moistened with a little cold water*
2 *tablespoons water*
1 *teaspoon sugar*
1 *teaspoon salt*

Pour a bit of oil in a wok (use an iron skillet if you don't have one) and fry the prawns till they change colour. Remove and put on a warm plate. Heat the oil; work in the cornflour; add the water, ginger, and black beans. Add the seasonings; heat thoroughly; pour the sauce over the prawns. Garnish with the onions.

142

SHRIMP TOAST

1½ lb shrimps, deveined and shelled
1 small onion
Pinch ginger
About 12 slices stale French bread
½ teaspoon sugar
1½ teaspoon salt
1 tablespoon cornflour, moistened with a little cold water
3 tablespoons water
1 pt safflower or corn oil

Chop the shrimps, then the onion; combine all the ingredients except the oil and spread on the bread. Heat the oil to very hot; deep-fry the bread on the shrimp side for several minutes; then turn and brown other side. Drain on paper towels and cut into small pieces. Serve immediately as an hors d'oeuvre.

CHINESE OMELETTE

This recipe could have many variations played upon it. I have included it in the Chinese section because Dr Dong showed me how to make it, but it's perfectly delicious as a breakfast omelette with herbs and parsley for filling, and I experimented once with several crushed cloves of garlic and came up with a great favourite of my husband's.

1 4¼-oz tin shrimps, or equal amount fresh
5 egg whites
3 tablespoons chopped Chinese cabbage and/or bean sprouts
Safflower oil to cover bottom of frying pan

Sauté the vegetables slowly in the oil, add the shrimps for another minute, and meanwhile break the egg whites into a bowl. Do not beat them! When the vegetables are tender, gently stir them into the egg whites in the bowl. When the mixture is well stirred, drop by the ladleful into the oiled pan, making small omelettes about 6 inches across. Use a spatula to keep them from spreading; they will take form almost immediately. Cook them slowly till brown; turn and brown on the other side. Meanwhile put 1 teaspoon cornflour in a bowl with a little cold water; add some soya sauce and a pinch of sugar; mix well. After the omelettes are removed from the pan, pour this mixture into it, and stir carefully till it becomes a clear, glaze-like sauce to serve over the omelettes.

SHRIMPS WITH VEGETABLES

2 *tablespoons corn oil*
1 *lb medium-sized raw shrimps, deveined and shelled*
1 *tablespoon soya sauce*
1 *clove garlic, crushed*
½ *teaspoon minced fresh ginger*
4 *stalks celery, thinly sliced*
1 *onion, thinly sliced*
6-*oz tin water chestnuts, thinly sliced*
¾ *lb fresh bean sprouts*
2 *tablespoons cornflour, moistened with a little cold water*
½ *teaspoon salt*
2 *tablespoons soya sauce*
½ *pt chicken broth*

Heat the wok and put in 1 tablespoon of the oil. When very hot put in the shrimps, soya sauce, garlic, and ginger. Stir 2 or 3 minutes until the shrimps turn nicely pink. Turn out on to the serving dish. Mix the cornflour, salt, soya sauce, and chicken broth. Reheat the wok, add the remaining oil, add the vegetables, chestnuts and the cornflour mixture, and simmer till the vegetables are done crisply. It will only take a few minutes. Pour everything over the shrimps and serve.

SHRIMPS AND CHICKEN WITH EGGPLANT

2 *chicken breasts*
$\frac{1}{4}$ *pt corn oil*
1 *large clove garlic, crushed*
1 *teaspoon grated fresh ginger*
1 *small aubergine (eggplant), unpeeled*
$\frac{1}{2}$ *lb small shrimps*
2 *tablespoons cornflour, moistened with a little cold water*
2 *tablespoons soya sauce*
6-*oz tin water chestnuts, sliced thickly*
3 *tablespoons chicken broth*
Chopped parsley

Cut the aubergine into sticks about the size of your little finger. Cover them with boiling water, cover the bowl, and let stand about 10 minutes. Drain well. Skin and bone the chicken breasts, slice the meat into pieces the same size as the aubergine sticks, and mix with the cornflour and soya sauce. Heat the wok; add the oil and then the garlic, ginger, and aubergine. Stir and toss until the aubergine is brown; then add the chicken mixture, shrimps, and chestnuts. Cook in the same manner until the chicken is done – it will only take a very few minutes. Add the broth, cook another minute, and serve sprinkled with the parsley. If desired, additional soya sauce may be served.

SHRIMPS WITH WALNUTS

2 *lb shrimps, shelled and cleaned*
1$\frac{1}{2}$ *pts water, salted*

145

½ *lb walnut halves*
2 *tablespoons cornflour*
3 *tablespoons soya sauce*
1 *green pepper, cut in strips*

Boil the shrimps in the salted water for 5 minutes; drain and save the liquid. Put the walnuts in a 450-degree or Reg. 8 oven for 4 or 5 minutes; then rub off their brown outer skins. Mix the cornflour with the shrimp water; add the shrimps, soya sauce, and green pepper. Cook for 3 minutes and add the nuts.

SHRIMPS AND GREEN PEAS

2 *lb shrimps, deveined and shelled*
¾ *lb peas*
½ *teaspoon powdered ginger*
1 *teaspoon sugar*
1 *teaspoon salt*
1 *teaspoon soya sauce*
1 *teaspoon cornflour*
3 *tablespoons cold water*
2 *cloves garlic, minced or crushed*
3 *tablespoons peanut oil*
3 *shallots, chopped*

Heat the oil in your wok, add the shrimps, and brown briskly. Remove the shrimps; add the shallots, ginger, garlic, and peas. Combine the cornflour, salt, sugar, and soya sauce in a smooth paste, thinning with the water, and add this mixture to the vegetables in the wok. Cook just till the peas are done, about 3 or 4 minutes at most, and add the shrimps. When everything is hot, serve immediately.

146

SHRIMP BALLS

2 lb shrimps, deveined and shelled
18 water chestnuts
1 tablespoon cornflour, moistened with a little cold water
2 teaspoons salt
½ teaspoon sesame oil
1 egg white
1 pt vegetable oil

Chop the shrimps very fine; chop the water chestnuts. Combine all the ingredients except the egg white and the vegetable oil. Heat this oil; form the shrimp-chestnut mixture into balls, dip them in egg white, and drop them into the oil. The balls will float when done, but fry till they are golden brown.

CANTONESE SOFT-FRIED CHOW MEIN

1 lb egg-free noodles (cellophane or pea starch, for instance)
3 tablespoons vegetable oil
1 tablespoon cornflour, moistened with a little cold water
3 tablespoons soya sauce
½ teaspoon sugar
½ teaspoon sesame oil
1 teaspoon salt
1 clove garlic, minced
1 thin slice ginger
½ lb crab, lobster, or shrimps
2 oz shredded or chopped bamboo shoots
2 oz bean sprouts, dried ends cut off
2 oz shredded or chopped celery
4 oz shredded or chopped Chinese cabbage
1 oz thinly sliced water chestnuts
2 oz Chinese mushrooms, soaked in cold water about 15 minutes, rinsed and cut up

147

6 *Chinese snow peas, cut diagonally into ¼-inch pieces*
2 *spring onions, minced*

Cook the noodles till almost done. Drain, rinse with cold water, and divide into two batches. Put 1 tablespoon oil in the wok and when hot fry half the noodles till slightly crisp; then fry the other half. Remove and place on a large serving dish.

Have ready beside the wok: the cornflour and water mixed with the soya sauce, sugar, and sesame oil; all the vegetables, and seasonings, and the seafood.

Heat the wok; over a high heat; add the remaining 2 tablespoons oil and the salt, garlic, and ginger. Add the seafood and stir for a few minutes; then add the bamboo shoots, bean sprouts, and celery, cabbage, water chestnuts, and mushrooms. Add ½ pt water; cover and cook for 3 minutes. Uncover and stir for 30 seconds. Next add the snow peas and thicken with the cornflour mixture. Stir in the spring onions; then add more sesame oil (after tasting to see if the flavour of sesame appeals to you). Remove from the heat, pour everything over the noodles, and garnish with Chinese parsley.

KOREAN BEAN SPROUTS

1 *lb bean sprouts*
2 *spring onions*
2 *tablespoons soya sauce*
2 *tablespoons roasted sesame seeds*
2 *teaspoons safflower or corn oil*
Salt

Wash fresh young bean sprouts in cold water, snipping off any dried-up ends. Cover with boiling water and cook for 3 minutes; drain. Cut the tops off the spring onions, slice

148

them into 1-inch lengths, and set aside. Chop the white part of the spring onions and add to the bean sprouts; also add the soya sauce, sesame seeds, and oil. Cook for 2 or 3 minutes; then add the sliced onion tops. Cook for 1 or 2 minutes, stirring frequently; add salt and serve as you would any vegetable.

BASS WITH BEAN SPROUTS

3–4 *pieces sea bass*
4 *oz chopped spring onions*
4 *tablespoons soya sauce*
1 *tablespoon slivered fresh ginger*
5 *tablespoons peanut oil*
½ *pt water*
1 *lb bean sprouts*

Put 3 tablespoons oil in the wok; when heated roll around to coat the wok and add the fish, the onions, 3 tablespoons soya sauce, the ginger, and the water. Cover the wok tightly, bring to a rapid boil, and allow to simmer about 45 minutes, or until the fish flakes easily. In the meantime, cook the bean sprouts in 2 tablespoons oil and 1 tablespoon soya sauce 5 minutes, put on a large platter, top with the steamed fish, and over this pour the remaining juices. Serve with rice and Chinese peas.

CHINESE-STYLE LOBSTER

3 1-*lb lobsters*
2 *tablespoons soya sauce*
1 *small onion, chopped fine*
2 *tablespoons water*

Split the lobsters lengthwise and clean well (I have this done at the fishmonger's). Place them on a rack either in a steamer or in your wok with a tight lid, with boiling water below. Mix the soya sauce, onion, and water and distribute on the lobsters; cover tightly and steam for 10 minutes. I almost prefer this to any other way of doing lobster, since it never gets tough. If you like, you can serve melted margarine, in addition, in a little pot beside each lobster half.

Since the Chinese don't go in for desserts, you might serve candied coconut, preserved ginger, dried litchi nuts, salted almonds, or cashews at the end of your Chinese dinner.

WOK-FRIED OYSTERS

2 *tablespoons corn oil*
1 *jar oysters (about 10 oz)*
2 *teaspoons soya sauce*

Pour the jar of oysters into a pan of simmering water and cook for 4 minutes. Drain. Heat the wok, add the oil, and when very hot add the oysters and soya sauce. Cook until the oysters' edges start to curl and they are done, about 3 minutes.

BEAN CURD AND SPINACH

Bean curd is made from our old friend the soyabean. It's known as the 'Wonderful Bean' in China, undoubtedly for the same reason that we treasure it. The curd is actually the moisture, or milk, from the soya bean. There are different textures – some soft, some hard. I suggest you experiment a little when buying it.

16 *pieces bean curd, about* 2 × 1 × 1 *inches*
½ *lb spinach cut in 2-inch pieces*
1 *teaspoon cornflour*
1 *clove garlic*
1 *tablespoon soya sauce*
½ *teaspoon salt*
1 *teaspoon brown sugar*
4 *tablespoons safflower or corn oil*

Cover the bean curd with water to which the salt has been added; soak 10 minutes; drain. Place 1 tablespoon oil in a flat pan and brown the bean curd carefully. You will find you can turn it over with the side of a knife. Add the soya sauce, sugar, and a little water; simmer 5 to 10 minutes. Now put 3 tablespoons oil in your wok and when hot toss in the spinach, garlic, and a little more salt. Stir and toss till almost done; add the bean curd and allow to cook without stirring for 1 or 2 minutes. Thicken with the cornflour (moistened with water) and serve. A few drops of sesame oil may be added if you like.

CREAMED CORN SOUP WITH CRAB

1-*lb tin creamed corn*
2 *oz crab meat*
2 *tablespoons cornflour, moistened with a little cold water*
Small quantity thinly sliced ginger or pinch powdered ginger
2 *tablespoons vegetable oil*
¼ *teaspoon salt*
1 *teaspoon sherry* (*this little bit can't hurt you*)
2 *pts water*
2 *egg whites, slightly whipped*

To the water add the ginger, sherry, oil, and salt; bring to a boil. Add the remaining ingredients, folding the egg whites in last. Serve very hot in Chinese bowls with china spoons.

151

Index